So you really want to learn

History:
Britain 1066-1500

So you really want to learn

History:
Britain 1066-1500

Bob Pace M.A.

Series Editor: Niall Murphy M.A. (Cantab)

www.galorepark.co.uk

GALORE PARK

Published by ISEB Publications, an imprint of Galore Park Publishing Ltd
19/21 Sayers Lane, Tenterden, Kent TN30 6BW
www.galorepark.co.uk

Typography by Typetechnique, London W1
Illustrations by Simon Tegg and Jane Humphrey

Printed by EuroGrafica S.p.A., Italy

ISBN-13: 978 1 905735 01 3

First published 2007

Details of other Galore Park publications are available at
www.galorepark.co.uk

ISEB Revision Guides, publications and examination papers may also be
obtained from Galore Park.

Foreword

So you really want to learn History: Britain 1066-1500 has been written to help you, the student, to understand something about the medieval past. You might ask questions such as: Why should I bother? How does it relate to my life? The world was very different before all the modern conveniences we take for granted. This was a world where turning on a light with the flick of a switch, getting water with the turn of a tap, or having entertainment at the push of a button was beyond the power of even the greatest of rulers. Perhaps you have noticed a strange name given to a street, or the unusual lumps in the ground at a park or field, or that so many people seem interested in old stone ruins of buildings. The study of history can start you on the path of discovery concerning these and many other things. For example – why Britain has a parliament and a monarch, why there is a Tower of London in the city of London, why there is a love-hate relationship between England and its neighbours of Wales, Ireland, Scotland and France or why so many people quarrel about the Middle East. These things that matter today are rooted in the past, and especially in the medieval past, as you will see.

The study of history as found in this textbook isn't just about facts and dates. It's about questioning and working out answers and seeing that there is more than one way to see events and ideas. The events in the medieval past are many hundreds of years old, but that doesn't make them less interesting; it makes them more challenging to understand, because so much information has been lost and the way people thought at the time can seem so foreign. At the same time, the people of the past are still people, in most ways like you and me, and their stories can tell us much about our world and ourselves. I hope you find this textbook the start of an involving and fascinating journey.

Publisher's note:

Words printed in red are defined in the glossary on pages 171-77

Acknowledgements

I would like to thank Nick Oulton of Galore Park and Jennie Williams of the Independent Schools Examinations Board for their encouragement to attempt this textbook. My thanks also go to Niall Murphy who has patiently edited this work. Last, but certainly not least, my thanks to my wife who has had to put up with weekends and holidays spent watching me toil away at this project.

Bob Pace, June 2007

The publishers are grateful for permission to use the photographs as follows:

(*T* = Top, *C* = Centre, *B* = Bottom, *L* = Left, *R* = Right.)

Cover © Lambeth Palace Library / Bridgeman Art Library; pp.1, 2, 5, 7T, 9, 12, 13 © Musée de la Tapisserie, Bayeux / Bridgeman Art Library; p.22 © Michael Nicholson / Corbis; pp.26, 27, 28 © British Library / Bridgeman Art Library; p.33 © World History Archive / TopFoto; p.34 © British Library / Heritage Images; p.38 © British Library / Heritage Images; p.39 © Mark Sutherland / photographersdirect.com; p.41BL, p.41BR, © British Library / Heritage Images; pp.47, 48 © British Library / Heritage Images; p.49 © Mary Evans Picture Library; p.51 © British Library / Bridgeman Art Library; p.53 © Lambeth Palace Library / Bridgeman Art Library; p.58 © British Library / Heritage Images; p.60 © Art Media / Heritage Images; p.62 © Bibliotheque Nationale, Paris / Bridgeman Art Library; p.64 © World History Archive / TopFoto; p.65 © Musée Conde, Chantilly / Bridgeman Art Library; p.70TL © British Library / Heritage Images; p.71 © Fontevrault Abbey / Bridgeman Art Library; p.72 © The Art Archive / Corbis; p.75 from Our Island Story by H.E.Marshall, published by Galore Park; p.78 © British Library / Heritage Images / TopFoto; p.79 © World History Archive / TopFoto; p.82TL © British Library / Bridgeman Art Library; p.82BR © English Heritage / Heritage Images / TopFoto; p.84T © Steven Vidler / Eurasia Press / Corbis; p.88TR © British Library / Heritage Images; p.88BL © World History Archive / TopFoto; p.91 © British Library / Bridgeman Art Library; p.93TL © Bibliotheque Nationale, Paris / Bridgeman Art Library; p.96 © Lambeth Palace Library / Bridgeman Art Library; p.99 © Bibliotheque Nationale, Paris / Bridgeman Art Library; p.100BL © English Heritage / Heritage Images / TopFoto; p.100BR © Steve Crampton / photographersdirect.com; p.104B © Dorling Kindersley; p.108 © Stapleton Collection / Bridgeman Art Library; pp.111, 113, 116 © British Library / Bridgeman Art Library; p.118 © British Library / Heritage Images; p.123 © Westminster Abbey / Bridgeman Art Library; p.125 © British Library / Heritage Images; p.129 © Westminster Abbey / Bridgeman Art Library; p.131 © Bibliotheque de l'Ecole des Beaux-Arts, Paris / Bridgeman Art Library; p.133 © Barnes Foundation, Merion, Pennsylvania / Bridgeman Art Library; p.135 © Bristol Records Office; p.136 © Philip Mould Ltd / Bridgeman Art Library; p.137 © World History Archive / TopFoto; p.138 © National Portrait Gallery, London / Bridgeman Art Library; p.142 © World History Archive / TopFoto; p.146 © Philip Mould Ltd / Bridgeman Art Library; p.147 © World History Archive / TopFoto; p.151 from Our Island Story by H.E.Marshall, published by Galore Park; p.154 © Bridgeman Art Library; p.157 © Philip Mould Ltd / Bridgeman Art Library; p.158 from Our Island Story by H.E.Marshall, published by Galore Park; p.161 © The Print Collector / Heritage Images.

Contents

Chapter 1 The Norman Conquest

Setting the Scene

Dawn's light on 15th October 1066 revealed a bloody sight. Thousands of men lay dead upon an English battlefield only a few miles from the sea. Amongst the dead were a great number of the most powerful men in England. One body was that of King Harold of England, but he was so badly cut up as to be almost unrecognizable. Moving amongst the dead were Norman soldiers looking for armour and weapons, and English families looking for their men. From the sea had come an invader who had staked everything on a quick and successful battle and had succeeded against the odds. But who was this invader? And why had he come?

Background

Some months before, on 5th January 1066, Edward the Confessor, King of England, died with no children to succeed him (see the family tree on page 166). This posed a major problem for the **Witan**, the council of important men of England, including **earls**, the greatest holders of land under the king, and the most important churchmen, the **bishops**. Edward's nearest male relative, Edgar the Atheling, was thought too young to be king, and it was the job of the Witan to find a successor and have him crowned king as quickly as possible.

Who should become king?

In the days and months that followed Edward's death, three men claimed that the throne should pass to them.

Harold Godwinson

Harold claimed that Edward had whispered on his deathbed that he, the most powerful earl of England and a proven warrior, should be the next to wear the crown of England. This scene is taken from the Bayeux Tapestry, a 70m long cloth embroidered in the 1070s on the orders of Odo of Bayeux, half-brother of William the Conqueror (see next page). Harold is talking to Edward on his deathbed, perhaps about who should be the next king.

Edward the Confessor's death; from the Bayeux Tapestry. The Latin reads: hic Eadwardus Rex in lecto alloquit(ur) fideles. Et hic defunctus est = Here King Edward in his bed speaks to his faithful companions. And here he died.

William, Duke of Normandy ('The Conqueror')

William felt he had been robbed of his inheritance, for he was a distant cousin of Edward the Confessor and claimed that Edward had promised, in 1052, that he should succeed him. Furthermore, in 1064, Harold Godwinson had been shipwrecked off the coast of France, captured by the local ruler Count Guy and then rescued by William. William claimed that before leaving, Harold had sworn an oath over the Normans' holiest **relics** that he would support William's right to the English throne. (Relics were objects that dated from the time of Christ, or once belonged to saints, and were believed to hold special power.) The Duke of Normandy felt that Harold had betrayed this promise and the scene is prominently depicted in the Bayeux Tapestry, for all to see.

Harold Godwinson swears an oath to Duke William; from the Bayeux Tapestry. The Latin reads: ubi Harold sacramentum fecit Willelmo duci = *Where Harold made an oath to Duke William.*

Harald Hardrada, King of Norway

Harald was well known for his ability as a warrior, and was nicknamed 'The Last of the Vikings'. He had the support of Tostig, Harold Godwinson's brother, who had lost his lands in England and was out for revenge. Since Viking kings had ruled England before, Hardrada began to raise forces to invade England from the north-east whilst Tostig took his forces and raided the English coast.

How do we know?

The three claimants to the throne all felt they had a strong claim. How do we know whose claim was the strongest? As historians, we have to look at the evidence.

A historian has to be very careful when looking at sources of information such as the scenes from the Bayeux Tapestry. How do we know that the source can be trusted? We need to ask, not only whether we think the information in the source is important, but also *who* produced the source, *when* it was produced and *why* it was produced. The answers to these three questions will help us decide how reliable the source is.

Harold Godwinson's claim

The *Anglo-Saxon Chronicle*, written by English monks living at the time, claimed that:

> the prudent King (Edward) had settled the kingdom on high-born men, on Harold himself, the noble Earl.

Similarly, the English monk, Florence of Worcester, wrote at the beginning of the 12th century:

> After Edward's burial, the under-king Harold, whom the king had named as his successor, was chosen king by the chief nobles of all England. He was crowned on the same day...

A historian would note that the writers of both these sources were English monks, one of whom was writing about forty years after the event. Is it possible that they might have been one-sided, or have had to rely on other writers for information?

William's claim

We have already seen how the Bayeux Tapestry depicts the scene in which Harold swears an oath to Duke William. William of Poitiers, a Norman soldier who later became William's priest, wrote the following:

> Edward loved William as if he was his brother or his son. He made William his heir and therefore sent Harold to William so that he could confirm this promise with an oath.

> Many truthful and honourable people who were there say that Harold swore on oath – of his own free will. He promised that he would do everything in his power to make sure that after the death of Edward, William would become King of England.

Again, a historian would note that the writer of the source, like the author of the Bayeux Tapestry, was Norman and worked for William of Normandy. The writer was not, in fact, at the battle but would have been able to speak to many who were there, particularly Normans. Because of this, and also because he wrote soon after the events, he certainly represents the views of the Normans at the time, and his account seems to confirm what we see in the Bayeux Tapestry. But is he balanced or one-sided?

Harald Hardrada's claim

The only evidence we have for Harald Hardrada's motives in invading England is from the *Heimskringla*, an anonymous collection of **sagas** about the kings of Scandinavia, written around 1225. According to the *Heimskringla*, Tostig convinced Hardrada of his claim to the English throne by saying that the King of Norway before Hardrada had an agreement with the King of England before Edward. The agreement was that if either died without children, the other would claim his kingdom. As Edward had not had any children, so Tostig argued, King Magnus should have then taken over the English throne, and Hardrada after him:

> King Harald thought carefully about the earl's words, and saw at once that there was truth in much of what he said; he also had a great desire to gain lands. Then King Harald and the earl talked long and frequently together; and at last he made the decision to go to England in the summer, and conquer the country.

This time the historian would note first that the writer of this source is anonymous (unknown), and secondly that a saga is a story meant to entertain, not necessarily to be accurate. Also the story was not written down for over one hundred and sixty years after the events. How much can we trust this source? This does not mean we cannot use it. Its use may not be so much to tell us the truth of the story, but rather how the Scandinavians viewed the story.

Every source has some use, but it depends upon what information is needed. Which of the sources used above gives us the most reliable information, and which tells us most clearly how each side felt?

Whether because they felt Edward had changed his mind about who should succeed him, or because it was easier to accept the claims of the man on the spot, the Witan chose the English-born Harold Godwinson as their new king and, the day after Edward's death, crowned him King Harold II.

The coronation of King Harold; from the Bayeux Tapestry. The Latin reads: hic residet Harold rex Anglorum = Here sits Harold, King of the English. Archbishop Stigand of Canterbury is also labelled (Stigant archieps).

Preparations

Harold knew that he would have to defend his new kingdom from both William and Harald Hardrada; and the spring and summer of 1066 were busy in Norway, Normandy and England as each side prepared for the coming clash. Harold had the most difficult task for his enemies could choose the time and place for their attack, while he could only watch and wait. In April, a shooting star, which we now know to have been Halley's comet, was spotted in the sky. People took this to be a bad omen. Having gathered his army, Harold decided to remain in the south of England to guard against a possible attack from William and left two earls, Edwin of Mercia and Morcar of Northumbria, to defend against the expected Viking attack in the north. As the summer drew to a close, however, Harold was under increasing pressure to allow his soldiers to return to their farmlands to gather in the harvest. As for the attackers, there was still no sign of them.

The English army

There were several different kinds of soldiers in the English armies of this time. The best-trained and equipped men were **housecarls** who were paid for by the king and the most important earls. At the other end of the scale were the **fyrd**, men who were usually farmers or worked in towns, but would fight when called upon. Some were nearly as well trained and equipped as housecarls, but most would have little armour and a few might not be armed with more than a knife or a club.

William of Normandy

William's early life had been difficult, even dangerous. He was the illegitimate son of Duke Robert of Normandy and Herlève, the daughter of a tanner. (An illegitimate child is one born to unmarried parents.) Only eight years old when his father died, William twice had to run for his life when attempts were made to murder him. He grew into a successful ruler, ruthlessly able to crush opposition and ambitious to increase his power.

William of Normandy had a number of major problems to solve before he could invade England. He had to win the support of his own reluctant **barons** who were the most powerful men in Normandy because of the land they held, make sure that his country would be safe from attack while he was gone *and* raise a large enough army to win. Many of the Norman barons were not keen to risk all on the invasion, although the chance of gaining more lands in England helped change many minds. To gain more support for his cause, he persuaded Pope Alexander II, the head of the Christian Church, that his invasion of England was right. This also made it much more difficult for his neighbours to consider attacking Normandy while he was gone.

The Church

Throughout this book you will be learning about the huge importance of the Christian Church. At this time people believed that, before Jesus died, he had entrusted his followers to Peter, one of his disciples. Peter came to be seen as the first leader of the Christian Church and his successors in this role were the **Popes**, based in Rome. The Pope was thus the leader of the Christian Church and had authority over all the leaders of the Church throughout Europe. Furthermore, because it was believed that kings received their authority to rule from God, Christian kings had a duty to respect the wishes of the Pope. The relationship between kings and the Church will be a constant theme throughout this book.

As William prepared his invasion force, he planned carefully. Many armies in the Middle Ages depended upon the area around them to provide their food, but William had enough supplies to last his force for many weeks. He did not strip Normandy of all its fighting men, but paid for troops from neighbouring areas such as Brittany. He had a mighty fleet of wooden ships made to take his army across the Channel to England but, when he gathered his army on the coast at Dives, the weather was against him. Without the right wind his fleet could not reach the English coast, so his army sat and waited.

The invasion fleet is built; from the Bayeux Tapestry

Harald Hardrada

The wind that kept William penned on the Normandy coast was the right wind to blow Harald Hardrada and his fleet of ships from Norway over to England. In September 1066, he and his army landed in the north of England. He then defeated the defending English army under Earls Edwin and Morcar at Fulford on 20th September, and went on to capture York.

Harold faced a critical decision in mid-September. His powerful army was stationed in the south of England, waiting to repel William. Should he remain in place in case William did appear, or should he risk marching north to face the invading army of Harald Hardrada? Should a king defend all his territory, or play safe and hold on to part of it? Harold had proved in the past that he was an able warrior and now he showed he could be daring too. He took his army and rapidly moved north, marching so quickly that he caught Harald Hardrada's invading Viking army by surprise near York.

The Battle of Stamford Bridge

On the morning of 25th September 1066, a cloud of dust was spotted by men in Harald Hardrada's army, who were waiting by Stamford Bridge for the citizens of York to deliver food and hostages. The dust cloud was coming from the direction of York and soon sparkles of light could be made out as sunlight reflected off the spears and helmets of Harold's approaching army. The Viking army was quickly thrown into confusion as men rushed to get ready and cursed the decision to leave their armour and two-thirds of their troops with their ships, nearly nine miles away. Hardrada led his army to higher ground across the river, leaving a few men to hold Stamford Bridge and slow the English army. Most of these men were quickly defeated, but on the bridge a lone Viking warrior stood and stopped the English, for the bridge was so narrow that the English could not overwhelm its single defender. Finally, one English soldier managed to cross the river, attack the Viking from behind and clear the way. However, the brave stand had served its purpose and the rest of Hardrada's army was now standing ready in a shieldwall (see below). Seeing this, King Harold's English army crossed Stamford Bridge and formed up in preparation for an assault.

Tactics in 1066

Armies of the eleventh century fought using weapons that caused soldiers to fight face to face and at very close range. Most armies had archers and slingers who would start the battle, but the decisive fighting would be done with spear, axe and sword. Both sides would form a **shieldwall** where men would stand close together and a number of ranks deep to present a solid front to the enemy. If a man fell in the front rank, another could step forward and take his place. Better-equipped warriors at the front of the shieldwall would wear ringmail armour, and metal helmets with a nasal piece to protect their nose. Wood and hide shields were commonly used, the Vikings favouring a round shape and the English using a mixture of round and kite-shaped shields. Most battles only lasted for a few hours, as the physical demands of combat would eventually sap the strength of even the strongest warrior.

The English charged into the Viking shieldwall and in the fighting both Harald Hardrada and Tostig were killed. Even the arrival of more Vikings from the ships made little difference and the surviving invaders were chased back to their ships.

The Normans land

King Harold had very little time to celebrate his victory. Within days of the battle he received news that William had sailed and had landed on the south coast of England. The Normans arrived at Pevensey on 28th September and, as we see in this picture from the Bayeux Tapestry, set about constructing a **motte and bailey** castle (see page 21) with materials which had been brought over with the invasion fleet. William sent his men through the countryside, seizing food, plundering and burning. Not only did the Duke need supplies but he had another reason for his actions. In order to achieve his aim of becoming King of England, William needed to smash the English army. If Harold could be encouraged to fight the Normans quickly, before recovering from the Battle of Stamford Bridge, this would play into William's hands.

Building a motte and bailey castle at Hastings; from the Bayeux Tapestry. The Latin reads (not all visible): iste iussit ut foderetur castellum at [ad] Hestenga = *He ordered a fort to be dug at Hastings. The fort is labelled* ceastra [castra] = *camp.*

Harold's decision

Harold's actions at this point are hard to understand. He had won an outstanding victory at Stamford Bridge but his forces were tired. He was also in the wrong place, nearly 300 miles away from the Normans. However, Harold decided to march south and reached London on 6th October, having marched 190 miles in eight days. His elite troops, the housecarls and **nobles** (the richest and most powerful men in England), had ridden with him but he had left the rest of his fyrd to follow on foot.

Harold's brothers, Gyrth and Leofwine, urged caution, saying that time should be taken to build up an overwhelming force to crush the Normans. But Harold was a man in a hurry, perhaps concerned that William would soon receive reinforcements, perhaps angered that his lands in southern England were being ravaged, or maybe just anxious to attack the Normans while they were near the sea and easy to defeat. Harold must also have been very confident after Stamford Bridge.

William of Normandy, however, was not about to be caught by surprise as Harald Hardrada had been. The English left London and marched for three days to reach William's army late on Friday 13th October. On the morning of 14th October, the men of Harold's army soon became aware that their Norman enemies were on the move and heading towards them.

The Battle of Hastings

How do we know what happened?

The Battle of Hastings was fought at a place called Senlac Hill, later to be named Battle, on 14th October 1066. What actually happened on that day is not very clear. No eyewitness recorded the event. Historians have a number of written sources and one pictorial source, the **Bayeux Tapestry**, from about this time to use. All but one of the sources from the time are Norman, and they do not agree with each other. The only English source, the *Anglo-Saxon Chronicle*, was not written by an eyewitness and gives very little detail concerning the battle. We can never be truly certain what actually happened, because the evidence is not entirely reliable. What follows is an account of the battle assembled from the different sources.

Before the battle

Harold had a core of elite housecarls and some experienced fyrd troops. However, he had to fill out his army with poorer local fyrd, as the majority of his troops from Stamford Bridge had no chance of arriving from the north in time for the battle. Harold took his position on top of Senlac Hill. His men formed a shieldwall nearly half a mile long and a number of ranks deep. To stiffen his poorer fyrd Harold placed groups of housecarls all along the line.

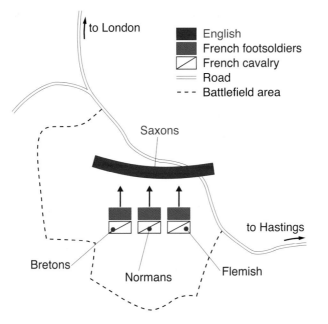

The Battle of Hastings, 14th October 1066

When Duke William had gathered his army in the valley below the English position, he formed it into three main sections. On the left were troops largely drawn from Brittany. In the centre were his men from Normandy, while on the right were the other hired soldiers. Each section had archers in the front, followed by foot soldiers. At the back of each section were the **knights**, men who fought on horseback with long spears called lances, perhaps numbering 2000 men. These knights also carried swords and sometimes axes. A few, like William and his half-brother Bishop Odo of Bayeux, carried maces, weapons very much like clubs. The entire Norman army was generally better-trained and equipped than the English, although the English housecarls were known throughout western Europe as great fighters.

The start of the battle

The battle started in the morning. The first major act of the fighting was when the Norman archers fired into the shieldwall. This would not have had much effect as they were shooting their arrows uphill at a group of men protected by shields.

Next the Norman foot soldiers marched up the ridge to attack the shieldwall. As they approached they were met with missiles, including spears, axes and even stones tied to sticks. Then they crashed into the English shieldwall. They would have encountered the full fury of the housecarls, using their two-handed axes with which they could easily split heads right through the helmets. The attack made no headway.

Then it was the turn of the Norman knights to advance as the foot soldiers drew back. The knights could throw javelins as well as use lances, but they must have been wary of the housecarls, who could bring down a horse with a single axe-blow. Again, Harold's shieldwall held firm, giving the knights no gaps to force their way in.

The Normans attack the shieldwall; from the Bayeux Tapestry

The turning-point

Some time during this furious combat the Breton soldiers on the left flank of the Norman army appear to have lost their appetite for fighting and began to retreat. Rumours were beginning to spread throughout the Norman forces that William had been killed. The entire Norman army began to fall back down the ridge, with the very real danger that this retreat could rapidly turn into a rout. William managed to encourage his knights in the valley by raising himself up, lifting his helmet off his head and shouting for his men to gather to him. This morale-boosting moment seems to have halted the Norman retreat. When some of the ill-disciplined English fyrd came running down off the ridge after the Bretons, they were met by Norman knights who slaughtered them easily.

This mistake may have cost Harold many of his best soldiers. Some Norman accounts claim that, encouraged by this, the Norman army now pretended to retreat in order to trick the English soldiers into rushing down the slope again. Whether this could be done by soldiers who shortly before had almost run away, or whether William could control his army like this in the midst of a major battle, is very uncertain.

How did the battle end?

Sometime during the afternoon Harold's brothers Gyrth and Leofwine were killed, which must have been a real blow to the king. His shieldwall still held firm, but had weakened in the face of constant Norman attacks. William launched a final attack in the late afternoon. This Norman attack brought the collapse of the shieldwall and the death of Harold. The Bayeux Tapestry appears to show Harold with an arrow in his eye, although we cannot be sure that this is really how he died. It is probable that he is represented by two figures on the Tapestry, first wounded by an arrow, then cut down by a Norman knight.

The death of King Harold; from the Bayeux Tapestry. The Latin reads: Harold rex interfectus est = *King Harold is killed.*

With his death, virtually all English resistance stopped as the fyrd scrambled to flee. On the battlefield lay the bodies of the three Godwinson brothers and most of the leading men of England.

Exercise 1.1

Answer each of the following questions with a full sentence:

1. Who died in January 1066?

2. Why was Edgar the Atheling considered unable to become king?

3. What kind of soldiers made up the English army at this time?

4. Which group of people did William have to convince before he could plan to invade England?

5. Who was defeated at Stamford Bridge?

6. Where did William set up a castle and wait for King Harold?

7. Where did King Harold's men set up their shieldwall on the 14th October 1066?

8. What kind of soldier did the Normans have that the English did not?

9. Which members of the Godwinson family other than Harold died at Hastings?

10. According to the Bayeux Tapestry, how was King Harold killed?

Exercise 1.2

List the three men who claimed the crown of England and give the main reason why each thought he should be king.

Exercise 1.3

Link the following events (1-10) with the dates (a)-(j), and write them out in the correct chronological (time) order:

1. Battle of Stamford Bridge.	(a) 6th January 1066
2. Edward promises the throne to William.	(b) 20th September 1066
3. Halley's comet seen.	(c) 28th September 1066
4. Harold is crowned.	(d) April 1066
5. The armies take up position on Senlac Hill.	(e) 5th January 1066
6. Battle of Hastings.	(f) 1064
7. Edward dies.	(g) 1052

8. Harold swears fealty to William.   (h) 14th October 1066

9. The Normans land at Pevensey.   (i) 25th September 1066

10. Battle of Fulford.   (j) 13th October 1066

Exercise 1.4

Read the two paragraphs below about the Battle of Hastings. They were both written by contemporaries, that is men who lived during the time, but neither was at the battle. Answer the questions which follow:

SOURCE A: Written by an English monk in a chronicle, known as the *Anglo-Saxon Chronicle*.

> *And William came against him by surprise before his army was drawn up in battle array. But the King nevertheless fought hard against him, with the men who were willing to support him, and there were heavy casualties on both sides. There King Harold was killed and Earl Leofwine his brother, and Earl Gyrth his brother, and many good men, and the French remained masters of the field, even as God granted it to them because of the sins of the people.*

SOURCE B: Written by William of Poitiers, who was a Norman soldier and a priest for Duke William.

> *Twice this trick [pretending to retreat] was used successfully, then the Normans attacked those who were left. The English army was still very strong but at last it weakened and the English suffered many deaths. Even the lightly wounded could not escape because the army was so tightly packed.*
>
> *As the daylight began to fade the English realised that they could not hold out much longer. They had lost most of their army, the King and two of his brothers were dead. The English turned and ran.*

1. Look at Source A. Give one reason why the English lost.

2. Look at Source B. Give several reasons why the English lost.

3. Look at both Source A and B. In what ways do they disagree about why the English lost?

4. Remembering how to use *who, when* and *why* (see How do we know? on page 3), how much can we trust these two sources? Explain your answer.

Essay questions

As historians, we will often be asked questions about the period of history we are studying. Different questions may be asked about the period, but you will often find that these are simply asking you to write down what you know in a variety of different ways. The important thing is to answer the question that has actually been asked.

In this book we will be learning how to answer essay questions, but here first are a few simple guides to help you. There are two types of essay question: those asking you to 'describe' (narrative essays) and those asking you to 'explain' (analytical essays):

Describe

- When you are asked to 'describe' an event or events, try to write as if you are telling a story. Structure your answer so that you have a sentence or two of introduction, a few paragraphs actually describing the events, and a sentence or two in conclusion.

- You need to make sure that your facts are accurate and in the correct order. Using the proper dates will show the examiner that you have remembered them, and earn you marks in an exam.

- Even though this is a story, you should not include personal opinion and you should write in the past tense.

Explain

- When you are asked to 'explain' something, don't waste time re-telling the story. Instead, you need to analyse the causes or consequences of the events about which you are writing.

- Remember that there will never be only one true answer, and that you will gain most marks for giving a balanced opinion. If you are asked whether an event was a success or a failure, for example, make sure you give reasons why it could be termed either way. Then in your conclusion you can weigh up which side has the most reasons. Useful starting words for this are 'On the one hand... On the other hand'.

- If you are asked to 'explain why an event happened' or 'explain its consequences', look at the different groups or categories of causes or results. This can be done by looking at short-term and long-term reasons or consequences, or by examining the different categories, such as money, power, the Church, etc. You may need to try to show how one cause or consequence is more important, and to do this it helps to see if causes or consequences link up or connect with each other.

- Always back your statements up with evidence, and use the historical sources that you have learned about. But make sure you say how reliable these sources are, and consider how this will affect your conclusion.

Exercise 1.5

1. Study the information in this chapter.
   (a) Make a list of every reason why William won and Harold lost the Battle of Hastings. Put them in order from most important to least important.
   (b) Explain in a paragraph why you placed the reasons in this order.

2. Consider the role played by either William or Harold Godwinson at the Battle of Hastings.
   (a) Describe the part he played in the events leading up to and during the battle.
   (b) Explain his success or failure during the battle.

3. Read the information in this chapter about war, armies and battles.
   (a) Describe the types of soldiers who took part in either the Battle of Stamford Bridge or the Battle of Hastings.
   (b) Explain why the winning side won.

Chapter 2 Conquered England

William I 'The Conqueror', 1066-1087

William the Conqueror was crowned King of England on Christmas Day, 1066, in Westminster Abbey. When the people inside were asked to cheer for him, the Norman soldiers outside thought there was trouble with the English and burnt down many of the surrounding buildings. Was William's rule always to be so violent?

To show his power to the English, Duke William had burnt and destroyed towns as he marched towards London from Hastings. Reluctantly, the English leaders who were still alive agreed to William being crowned. But might they still decide to rebel?

Medieval rule and the Feudal System

There were over a million people living in England and William only had a few thousand soldiers. He needed to be in control and, most importantly, he needed his barons to support him. This is why the **Feudal System** was so important. At this time, people believed that all the land in a kingdom was given to the king by God. To help rule the country, the king kept some land and gave the rest of it to his **tenants-in-chief**. These were the most powerful of the barons and churchmen; they received the food and rent from this land and controlled the people who lived on it. But in return for this gift of land, the king wanted these men to serve him loyally and to provide soldiers for his army. The tenants-in-chief had to pay **homage** to the king by kneeling before him and swearing **fealty** to him as loyal **vassals**. The oath of fealty involved the vassal promising to defend his lord in war by providing a certain number of armed men, depending on the amount of land he held, whenever required. But where would these men come from?

To collect the armed men that they had promised to the king, the tenants-in-chief gave land to lesser people, knights, and in return these knights paid homage to the tenants-in-chief. The knights in turn gave land to people below them, such as **yeoman** farmers, in return for their service. This system, the Feudal System, ensured that everyone below the king had a **lord**, to whom he owed fealty. The higher up the ladder you were, the more you had to promise to provide to your lord in time of war. At the bottom of the ladder, a humble **freeman** promised to come in person to the defence of his lord. This lord brought all freemen who had sworn fealty to him to the defence of *his* lord. This lord brought these men to the defence of *his* lord, and so it went on, right up to the king at the top of the ladder. In this way the king could be sure of raising an army when he needed one.

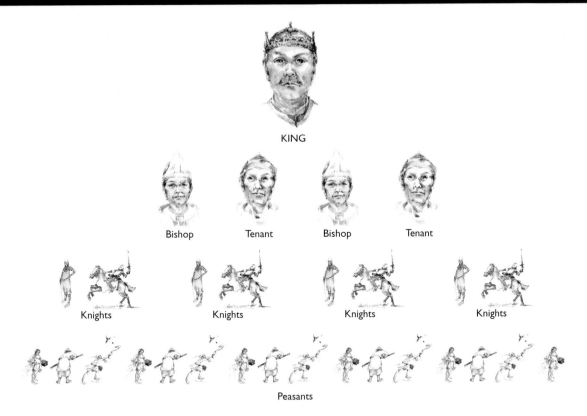

KING

Bishop   Tenant   Bishop   Tenant

Knights   Knights   Knights   Knights

Peasants

The Feudal System

Lord – the man who gave land in exchange for military service.

Vassal – the man who received the land in exchange for military service.

Homage – the physical act of kneeling in front of your lord to receive your land.

Fealty – the oath a vassal made to his lord, promising his loyalty, when paying homage.

In a collection of laws and customs made in 1180, this is how the relationship between lord and vassal was described:

> *Homage means that the person becomes the lord's man and shall be loyal to him and uphold his honour, unless this goes against his duty to the king. It is obvious that a man will break his oath of homage if he injures his lord, except in self-defence or if the king raised an army against his lord.*

Revolts and rebellions

At first, William tried to keep the English on his side and let men like the English earls Edwin and Morcar keep their lands after swearing loyalty to him. He soon regretted his decision as, up and down the country over the next few years, Englishmen revolted against his rule. The most dangerous of these revolts was in the north of England in 1069 when English rebels, including the earls Edwin and Morcar, received support from an invading force of Vikings and Scots. The Norman defenders of York were all killed by these rebels. William was furious and, after re-taking York, he decided to teach his English subjects a lesson they would not forget. His army was sent through the north, killing and burning everything in its path. This was known as the **Harrying of the North** and left areas such as Yorkshire a wasteland. Unable to grow their crops, many people in these areas died of hunger. Most of the English rebellions stopped after this.

Orderic Vitalis was a half-English, half-Norman chronicler who mostly supported William's actions. But he was nonetheless shocked by the Harrying of the North:

> I have often praised William before, but I cannot for this act, which caused both the innocent and guilty alike to die by slow starvation... Such brutal slaughter cannot go unpunished.

One man who refused to give up the fight was **Hereward the Wake**. Hereward became a hero to the conquered English through the stories of his fight against the Norman invaders. He hid in the marshlands of East Anglia and defeated the Normans again and again. The story goes that, when William himself finally tracked Hereward down, the English hero killed his horse rather than let the Normans take it. We are not sure what happened to Hereward: some say he escaped; others that he died and some even believe that William allowed him to go free.

New buildings

To help with the process of keeping their new people under control, the Normans introduced a new kind of building to England: the **castle**. What William and his barons needed was a protected living area and a place to keep soldiers, especially knights, to control their new lands. The first castles were almost all motte and bailey castles made of wood. This kind of castle used cheap local materials and could be built quickly without the need for skilled labour. In fact, the local people were usually forced to help build the castle. The site of the castle was important, and it was often built at a river crossing or where it would overlook an important road or waterway. As you can see in the picture opposite, ditches and banks of earth were a vital part of a motte and bailey castle. Usually, the people living in the castle, including a baron's family, would have living quarters in the bailey. There needed to be housing for the soldiers who defended the castle and stables for the horses of the knights. Just as important was the hall built for the owner of the castle and there might also be a chapel. The bailey would be surrounded by a wooden wall and around this would be a deep ditch, making it even more difficult for an attacker to break in. However, if this did happen the defenders could retreat to the motte, a steep man-made hill with a tower on top, where they would try to hold out until help arrived.

An artist's impression of a motte and bailey castle

Of course, the wooden motte and bailey castles had their weaknesses. They would rot after twenty to thirty years. More importantly, they could be attacked by fire. However, no castle could survive long without a well, so there was always water to drink and with which to fight fire, and the earthworks of the castle could still cause the attackers problems, even once the walls had rotted.

Over the twenty years following the Battle of Hastings the Normans began to settle into England. Because of the English revolts, almost all the lords of the land were replaced by Normans. In the Church, most of the bishops were replaced by Normans, and they began a programme of rebuilding the churches and cathedrals in the Norman manner, with thick stone walls, small windows and rounded arches. The picture on page 22 shows Rochester Cathedral, built by the Normans in the twelfth century.

Rochester Cathedral; an example of a Norman cathedral

The Domesday Book

Perhaps nothing showed William's desire to control his new country more than the making of a country-wide survey, the results of which were recorded in the **Domesday Book**. William wanted to collect this information for a number of reasons, including the following:

- he feared another Viking invasion and needed to know where he could station and feed his soldiers;

- he thought that some of his barons might be holding lands that should belong to him or the Church; and

- he wanted to be able to collect more taxes.

So, at Christmas 1085 William sent his men out to survey the land by asking the local people of each farming unit (or manor) a number of questions.

Imagine being called together to speak to a small group of visiting French pupils who want to know things like: 'What is your history teacher like? Who was your teacher last year? Who was your teacher in Year 3? How much school kit do you own now?

How much did you have in Year 3?' The problem is that these French pupils do not speak English and their teacher has to pass questions and information back and forth.

This was very much the situation English villagers faced in 1086 when Norman officials appeared in order to ask questions to write the Domesday Book. We learn in a draft survey taken in Cambridgeshire, for example, that William's commissioners wanted to know:

> The name of the manor; who held it in King Edward's time; who holds it now; how much land there is; how many ploughlands belong to the domain and how many belong to the men; how many villeins, cottars, slaves, freemen and sokemen; how much woodland, pasture, meadow; how many mills or fisheries; how much has been added to the estate or taken away; what it was worth and what it is worth now. All this is to be recorded for three periods: as it was in King Edward's time; as it was when King William granted the manor; and as it is now.

It must have been both strange and frightening, for the Normans (with their different language) were now the lords of the land and had to be obeyed. The answers they were given were noted down and sent to Winchester where they were written down on parchment and collected together into a book. The result of this survey, the Domesday Book, was the first wide-ranging survey of England and it still exists in the National Archives. It allows us to have a glimpse of what life must have been like for the English in 1086, and it is a very useful historical source.

Compiling the Domesday Book: a modern interpretation

The manor

At the time of the Domesday Book, almost all English people lived in the countryside as farmers. As we shall see, farming methods of the time provided just about enough food in good years, if nearly all the population worked on the crops. Norman lords owned the land because they had been granted it as part of the Feudal System. The farming unit was the **manor**, which was made up of fields of crops, woods, meadows and a village. No one manor was the same as another because of the geography of the land, and a manor might contain more than one village or only half a village. However, all the villagers had to work for and obey the lord, who could be anybody from the king or the Archbishop of Canterbury down to a simple knight.

All sorts of peasants, that is, simple farmers, lived on a manor. Freemen, who were not tied to the land like the others, tended to be the wealthiest. Next were the **villeins** or **serfs**, who had land to farm but were not free to leave the manor. Beneath them were **cottars**, unfree 'cottage holders' who had little or no land to farm. Worst off were the slaves, although these were soon to disappear with the new Norman rulers. It is difficult to see where women fitted into this system as they are hardly mentioned at all in the Domesday Book. It is likely that higher-class women would have enjoyed some benefits of their husband's position, but would only very rarely have had land of their own. One such exception was a lady called Asa, from Scoreby in Yorkshire, who the Domesday Book records as holding land 'separately from her husband Bjornulfr, even when they were together'. Theirs must have been an unhappy marriage!

A modern artist's idea of a manor at the time of the Domesday Book

The village of a manor contained a number of houses or cottages, many of which had a **croft**, a large garden extending to the back. Here the villagers grew vegetables and kept animals such as bees, chickens, geese, goats and sheep. This was all the land a cottar had on which to grow food. The houses were made by the peasants from the materials locally available, which often meant **timber-framed** and **wattle-and-daubed** buildings (see page 130) with only one or two rooms. The floor was earth and any furniture was homemade. On the floor was a hearth for the fire and a gap would be made somewhere in the (usually thatched) roof to allow the smoke to escape. Windows were very small and closed off by a wooden shutter, as glass was a luxury for the very rich. In the winter especially, the house was shared between people and the most important animals, such as oxen and sheep, which would keep the house warm; but imagine the smell!

The most important building in a village was its **church.** Made of stone, this might be the only long-lasting structure in the village. As we shall see later, it played a key role in village life. (See Chapter 3)

Some manors would have another important building: a **manor house**. This would be the home of the lord of the manor when he was visiting, for many lords held a number of manors and continually travelled between them. If the manor was owned by an abbot or other churchman it was unlikely he would ever live or even visit there. Instead, a steward would look after the land on his behalf.

Farming the land

The farming year followed a pattern that depended upon the seasons. In the spring, ploughing the great open fields was a key job and peasants would share their oxen to help pull the ploughs. In much of England, open-field farming was used. Instead of a number of small, fenced or hedged fields, the land was divided into two or three huge fields. Each of these was organised into long strips, wide enough to allow a team of oxen to turn when ploughing. The freemen and villeins would hold a number of individual strips that would be dotted all over each field, so that everybody received a fair share of both better and poorer soil. Many of the strips would belong to the lord of the manor and would be known as his **demesne**. Ploughing of the demesne was done either by villeins as part of their service to their lord, or by cottars for wages. Each year, one of the huge fields would be left **fallow** (i.e. to rest). It would be ploughed, but no crop would be planted, and very soon grass and weeds would begin to grow on it. Over the spring and summer the villagers would allow their animals to graze there and even add to the manure their animals left with extra from their crofts. Then the fallow field would be ploughed in autumn or spring and be ready for a new crop to be sown. This job wasn't just for the men. The man would usually guide the plough while his wife might goad the oxen on or follow behind, crushing big lumps of clay soil with a wooden mallet, or scattering seeds.

A peasant ploughing; from the Luttrell Psalter, a 14th century illustrated book

Other parts of the manor's lands had various important uses. Some land was set aside as meadow so that long grass could grow and be harvested as hay for the animals. Woodlands were very important as they provided materials for houses and furniture, fuel for the hearth and food in the form of acorns for pigs. Some land was held in common, where the peasants could allow their animals to graze. The word 'common' today still refers to an area of land which was shared in this way. Clapham Common is just one famous example.

Summer would mean a great many jobs to do, so the villagers would work from dawn until dark. Weeding and tending of crops, looking after cattle and pigs, haymaking, working in the woods and cleaning and tending ditches were just some of the chores expected of every farmer. Harvesting of corn and other crops might start in mid-summer and extend well into autumn. Then it was time to start ploughing again for a crop of spring corn, and also killing some of the livestock (and preserving the meat), for only a few animals would be able to survive the winter months. During all this labour villeins not only tended their own crops and animals, but also spent several days each week working on their lord's land for nothing. Cottars had to depend upon earning a wage by working for others in order to provide enough food for their families.

gaudebunt campi ⁊ omnia que in eis sunt.

Harvesting; from the Luttrell Psalter

Work did not stop in the winter. The corn that had been harvested needed to be threshed to separate seed from stalk. The grain was then divided amongst the farmers of the open field for, while each looked after his strips, the harvesting process was carried out by the whole village: men, women and children gathered the crop together. During the winter weather the farming families were occupied with indoor tasks: while the men would sharpen tools, thresh the corn and do general repairs, the women might spin wool and sew clothes for the family.

The kind of crops grown depended upon the region of England. The south, East Anglia and some of the Midlands grew wheat, barley and beans in their open fields. In the south-west, small enclosed fields were more common and people tended to live in very small villages or hamlets, or even in individual farmsteads. In the north, farming involved the raising of animals such as sheep, although oats were a common crop. At the time of the Domesday Book, however, much of the north was listed as wasteland. This might just mean land that wasn't ploughed and was used for meadows, but the events of 1069 (see page 20) might also have been the reason.

Food and entertainment

The kind and amount of food English peasants ate at the time of the Domesday Book depended upon who they were, where they farmed and the season. Early spring was usually a very hungry time even when the harvests had been good, as the stored food began to run out or rotted. For most villagers their main foods would be bread and a form of thick soup called **pottage**. Meat was rarely eaten, as the villagers' animals were kept to provide things like eggs, wool, milk and labour. This meant that most of the ingredients of pottage would be vegetables and grain, such as barley, turnips and carrots that the villager grew in his croft. As well as helping their husbands in the fields, women were expected to cook for their families and take care of the vegetable garden. A day's meals might start with bread and weak beer in the morning, with the same at lunchtime, perhaps with some cheese. The evening meal would be pottage. Ale or beer was drunk because water was thought to make people ill, although the reason for this was not understood. Milk, usually goat's or sheep's, was much more valuable for making cheese and butter than as a drink. A drink for children would be the thin liquid, called whey, left over from turning milk into cheese.

A peasant's life was one of hard labour. Because of this and the quality of their diet, it is not surprising to learn that most peasants did not live often beyond the age of about forty. Children were expected to help with work as soon as possible, which might mean young boys chasing birds away during planting and girls helping their mothers with cooking and spinning wool. There was very little chance for schooling, and little opportunity to do anything other than work on the land. The villagers were given days off from work, however, including every Sunday. There were also about twenty holy days each year, including Christmas, Easter and Whitsuntide (the seventh week after Easter). At Christmas sometimes the lord of the manor would hold a great feast and the villagers would be given bread and meat and plenty of ale to drink.

A medieval feast; from the Luttrell Psalter

On May Day there would be dancing around the maypole and at Midsummer's Eve a bonfire feast. An early form of football was played between different villages, involving as many as a hundred or more players, and sometimes resulting in players being badly hurt. Not surprisingly, some lords banned football in their manors.

Exercise 2.1

Write out the following paragraphs, filling in the blanks from the information in this chapter:

William I used a number of different methods to control England. He used the _____ System, where the king gave land to _____-in-_____ in exchange for _____ to fight wars or rebellions.

When a rebellion broke out in the north of England, William punished the people there by the _____ of the _____. The English made a hero of one rebel, _____ ___ _____.

The Normans worked to hold on to their conquered land by building _____. The most common type at first was the _____ and _____. They also rebuilt many of the English _____.

In 1085 William ordered a survey of the land to be taken, the results of which were recorded in the _____ Book, to find out, among other things, how much _____ he should be paid.

Exercise 2.2

Write a few sentences about each of the following:

1. The Feudal System

2. Tenants-in-chief

3. Homage and fealty

4. Hereward the Wake

5. The Harrying of the North

6. Motte and bailey castles

7. Norman churches

8. The Domesday Book

Exercise 2.3

Write out the paragraph below, filling in the blanks using the information from pages 24-27:

The _____ was the unit of farming in much of England. Each was held by a _____. Most of the people who lived there were _____, or simple farmers. Most would live in a small house that was _____-framed and raise vegetables in their _____. The main crops were grown in the _____ _____, which were divided into strips. The lord of the manor's land was called the _____.

Exercise 2.4

Copy the picture of the manor on page 24, then label the following:

church	manor house	croft
woods	common land	peasant's house

Exercise 2.5

Using the information from this chapter, write a paragraph describing a day in the life of a peasant. Be careful to write whether the peasant is a freeman, villein or cottar; a man or a woman and what time of year it is.

Exercise 2.6

Read the following sources about ploughmen and then answer the questions:

SOURCE A: From Geoffrey Chaucer's *The Canterbury Tales*. Chaucer wrote these stories in the late 1300s.

> There was a ploughman with him there, his brother;
> Many a load of dung one time or other
> He must have carted through the morning dew,
> He was an honest worker, good and true,
> Living in peace and perfect charity...
> For steadily about his work he went
> To thrash his corn, to dig or to manure
> Or make a ditch; and he would help the poor
> For love of Christ and never take a penny

If he could help it, and, as prompt as any,
He paid his tithes in full when they were due
On what he owned, and on his earnings too.

SOURCE B: From William Langland's *Piers Plowman.* Langland was a minor churchman who wrote his poem at about the same time that Chaucer was writing.

As I went by, I saw a poor man hanging on to a plough. His coat was of coarse material. His hood was full of holes, and his hair stuck out of it. As he trod the soil, his toes stuck out of his worn shoes with their thick soles. His hose hung about his legs on all sides. He was daubed with mud as he followed the plough. He had two mittens made of rough stuff, with worn-out fingers and thick with muck. This man sank almost to his ankles as he walked in the mud. To pull his plough he had four heifers. They were so feeble and thin that you could count their every rib, so sorry-looking were they.
His wife walked beside him with a long goad (to drive the oxen). She walked barefoot on the ice, so that the blood flowed.

(a)   Look at Source A. Name the jobs this peasant did.

(b)   Look at Source A. What does the source tell us about whether the peasant was poor or not?

(c)   Look at Source B. Who is working in the field and what are they doing?

(d)   Look at Source B. How does Langland show whether the peasants are poor or not?

(e)   Look at the Luttrell Psalter picture of ploughing on page 26. How does this picture agree or disagree with Sources A and B? Make sure to explain your answer, saying clearly what the picture shows and comparing it with the written sources. Use quotations from the sources to make your points.

Exercise 2.7

Read the following extract from the *Anglo-Saxon Chronicle*, a history written by English monks during the time.

If anyone wants to know what sort of man he [King William] was, what were his achievements or what land he held – then I (who once lived at his court and saw him often) will tell of what I know.

King William was a very wise man, very powerful and more honoured and stronger than any previous English king. He was kind to those who loved God, and completely ruthless against those who opposed him...

He was a very stern and violent man, so that no one dare oppose him. He put earls in prison, dismissed bishops and abbots... and even punished his own brother, Odo...

We must remember the law and order he established, so that any honest man could travel safely even if he was carrying gold; and no one dared kill another person however much they had been wronged...

In his time, there was much oppression and very great distress. He built castles and heavily oppressed the poor; he was extremely hard and unjustly took from his subjects large amounts of gold and silver – which he did not need: it was pure greed. He formed vast royal forests for hunting and ordered poachers to be blinded.

What kind of man was William, Duke of Normandy and King of England? Make a table of two columns, one labelled 'William's good points', the other 'William's bad points'. Use the information in the first two chapters and the source above to fill in your table.

Chapter 3 The sons of William I

William the Conqueror had three living sons at his death and two of them would rule England (see the family tree on page 167). Only Robert, the eldest son, would never be King of England.

William II, 1087-1100

William II, or 'Rufus' (the Red), was the second son of William the Conqueror. He ruled England for thirteen years. He was a strong king who crushed rebellions, including one led by his brother Robert, the Duke of Normandy, and fought against the Welsh and Scots. His greatest wish was to rule Normandy as well as England and this he managed in the end by lending Robert money to go on the First Crusade. This crusade was an attempt by Christian Europe to take Jerusalem and other parts of the Middle East recently captured by Islamic invaders (see Chapter 5).

William Rufus had a foul temper and did not seem to be very concerned about the Church, which was a real problem in a time of strong religious beliefs. When the most important man in the Church in England (the Archbishop of Canterbury) died, Rufus did not replace him for years, instead using the Church's wealth himself. Only in 1093 did he finally appoint a replacement. The new archbishop, Anselm, did not get along well with William and the two argued over who was really in charge of the Church in England, the king or the Pope. Anselm left England in 1097 because of these arguments and Rufus took the opportunity to seize more Church lands and money.

In 1100 William Rufus was killed. He had been hunting in the New Forest with several other men when he was hit by an arrow and died. Blame fell on a man called Walter Tyrrel who fled the scene, no doubt afraid of being charged with the King's murder. It may have been a tragic accident; we will never know for sure. However, William's younger brother Henry who had also been hunting at the time, moved very quickly to take the crown for himself. With his older brother Robert still involved in the First Crusade and unable to prevent him, Henry became Henry I, King of England.

The death of William Rufus; from a 19th century children's history book

Henry I, 1100–1135

The youngest son of William the Conqueror was quite different from his brothers. He was not the great fighter they were, being happier to command from the back than the front. Henry could also be very cruel and ruthless, once having two of his granddaughters blinded because their father had done the same to hostages he was holding. Yet he also became known as 'The Lion of Justice' because of the work he did to spread royal justice throughout England, and he helped encourage learning.

Henry faced many problems during his thirty-five year rule.

Henry I, youngest son of William I; from a manuscript produced around 1200

- His brother Robert, Duke of Normandy, returned from the First Crusade and claimed he was the rightful King of England.

- His barons in France were not always very loyal.

- The King of France tried to take his lands in Normandy from him.

- He needed to heal the split with the Church caused by his brother.

- In 1120 his son was drowned when his ship (the *White Ship*) sank in the Channel, leaving only Henry's daughter Matilda to take the throne after him.

So, how did Henry solve his problems? He dealt with his brother Robert by defeating him in battle and keeping him locked up as a prisoner for the rest of his life. His barons certainly caused him problems but he crushed all rebellions against him. And, while his enemies in France cost Henry much time and money, he managed to hold on to Normandy.

Henry realised that he needed the support of the Church and brought Archbishop Anselm back from exile in 1100. (Being 'in exile' means being forced to leave your country.) He did much to encourage the growth of monasteries, places established for monks, in England and even made one churchman, Roger, Bishop of Salisbury, his most important official. However, Henry did quarrel with Archbishop Anselm about who should appoint new bishops and abbots (the heads of monasteries). The Church, led by the Pope in Rome, claimed that it should be the Church, while Henry I believed that it should be kings who appointed these important men. He argued that they were not just Church leaders, but also great landholders in the Feudal System and, like Roger of Salisbury, could also be important government officials. In the end, a compromise was reached, that the king would choose a person for the position and the Church would then officially 'elect' this person. Outwardly the Church appeared to choose the bishop or abbot, but the king had the major say in the choice. This is how the Church and king were to work together for most of the Middle Ages.

Henry enjoyed much success during his rule. However, the problem of who would become the next ruler was to cause a great deal of trouble.

What made a good king?

There were a number of ideas at the time about what made a good king:

- He should be a brave warrior, capable of leading his soldiers to victory in battle.

- He should support and protect the Church, as it was God who made him the king.

- He should be just and fair and listen to the views of the important men of his kingdom.

- He should make sure that he left an adult son to rule after him.

The trouble with Matilda

Girls born to noble families in the Middle Ages were expected to be educated and prepared for marriage. They usually had a husband chosen for them by their parents for the economic or political advantage of the family while they were still babies, and they could be legally married from the age of twelve. These girls were usually educated at a nunnery, where they were taught not only to read and appreciate literature and music, but also the manners, speech and fashions that would be expected of them once they were married. They might also be sent into the care of an educated woman who would teach them to imitate her style and behaviour.

In spite of this the belief held by men and many women was that a woman was unfit to hold any formal political power. This belief was to cause major problems concerning who should rule England and Normandy after Henry I. Henry had twenty children born outside his marriage, but only one surviving legitimate child, his daughter Matilda. Henry tried to go against the beliefs of his time by having Matilda inherit the crown from him. He tried hard to make his reluctant barons agree to this. He also arranged for Matilda, who had been married (at the age of thirteen) to the Holy Roman Emperor and then widowed, to marry sixteen-year-old Geoffrey Plantagenet, who would one day rule Anjou in France. Geoffrey did not prove very loyal either to Matilda or her father, and in fact Henry I died in 1135 while fighting against him in France.

Exercise 3.1

Write out the following paragraphs and fill in the blank spaces, using the information from the chapter:

William I left three sons when he died, _____, _____ and _____. Only _____ was never to rule England. William II was very successful at crushing _____ and managed to rule _____ when his brother Robert went on _____. However, William II quarrelled with Archbishop _____ and was killed while hunting in the _____ _____.

Henry I sorted out the problem of Normandy by capturing and locking _____ up. He made peace with Anselm, but they later _____ over who should choose _____ and abbots. However, he encouraged the building of _____. Henry's biggest problem was who would follow him when his _____ drowned. His daughter, _____, was next in line.

Exercise 3.2

Write a few sentences about each of the following:

1. William II

2. Archbishop Anselm

3. Robert, Duke of Normandy

4. The *White Ship*

5. Roger, Bishop of Salisbury

6. Matilda

7. Geoffrey Plantagenet

Exercise 3.3

1. Write as a title 'William II' and then make two lists underneath, one headed 'Successful', the other 'Unsuccessful'. Using the ideas from page 35 on what made a good king, write down in your lists your assessment of William II during his rule.

2. Do the same thing as question 1 with Henry I.

3. Was William II or Henry I the more successful king? Use the lists from questions 1 and 2 either to hold a class debate, or write a four-paragraph essay using the writing frame below:

   Who was the more successful king, William II or Henry I?

   I think that _____ was the better king.

   Both kings were successful in some ways. William II was a good ... He also ... Henry I was successful in ... He was also good in ...

   However, both kings had their failures. William II was not very good at ... and Henry I was poor at ...

   Although both kings had successes and failures, I believe that the more successful was _____. This is because ...

How important was the Church?

As we have seen, the Church was much more than simply a stone building by the side of a village green. It was made up of thousands of people, both men and women, throughout Europe. Some of the men in the Church were the equals of barons and even kings. The Roman Catholic Church was the only church for the people of Europe and its ideas about the world were what people at that time believed.

One of the most important aspects of medieval Christian belief was the firm conviction that if one did anything to displease God, or indeed the Church, one ran the serious risk of going to Hell. Fear of Hell was a major factor in encouraging people to fall in line with the Church's teachings and to obey the will of God. And because most people could not read, one easy way to remind them of the danger of going to Hell was to paint frightening pictures on the walls of churches. Turn the page and you will see a typical medieval depiction, full of burning fires and horned devils.

Look carefully at the picture below. Imagine that you are standing in the middle of this scene. What might you hear, smell, feel?

A medieval vision of Hell; from the Bedford Missal, produced in 1423

Pictures like this were painted on the walls of village churches. It would be one of the very few pictures the villagers would ever see. (Imagine no TV, books, magazines, PlayStation or cinema.) The priest would explain that unless the people believed and followed their religion they would go to Hell. Villagers were also told about Heaven, a paradise they could reach by being good Christians.

Every Sunday, medieval people went to church to see these pictures and others of Jesus, his mother Mary and other holy people. They were told stories from the Bible and listened to Mass, the main service of the church day, but very few would have understood this service, as it was said in Latin.

The Church in local life

The village church was at the centre of village life. Its priest would baptise the village babies in a ceremony to ensure that they were accepted into the Church and to prevent their souls from going to Hell after death. The priest would also marry couples and bury the dead in holy ground. A good priest would also visit the sick, look after the poor and perhaps teach a few of the brightest boys how to read and write.

The church building was the centre of social life, its churchyard used for sports, festivals and meetings. Saints' days and religious festivals provided everybody with holy days off work (the origin of our 'holidays').

Durham Cathedral, an example of a Norman cathedral

The Church's wealth and power

All the local churches and their priests were grouped by area, or **diocese**, to be organised and led by a **bishop**. This high-ranking churchman would be based in a **cathedral**, a much larger building than a village church, that showed the power of the bishop.

The bishop would be a great landowner, like a baron, and might even raise soldiers in time of war. For example, Bishop Odo, William the Conqueror's half-brother, fought at the Battle of Hastings. The Church also raised its own taxes, called **tithes**, giving bishops the chance to control great wealth and to live in palaces next to their cathedrals.

Organising and leading the bishops were the **archbishops**. In England there were two: the Archbishop of Canterbury who was the leader of the Church in England, and the Archbishop of York. These two men were very powerful, often working for the king. Every once in a while an archbishop could prove a real problem for a king, as Archbishop Anselm did for William II.

The clergy of the Roman Catholic Church, from the poorest priest to the mightiest archbishop, were meant to listen to and obey the man who led the entire Church, the Pope. Usually the Pope's home was Rome, but at times Popes lived elsewhere, for example in France. There were sometimes arguments over who should have the title, as whoever was Pope controlled a church of great wealth and power throughout most of Europe. At one point three different men all claimed to be Pope at the same time! Even kings could not always have their own way against the Pope.

The other Church – monasteries and nunneries

Priests, bishops, archbishops and popes all worshipped God and were meant to follow strict rules. But these men also took part in everyday life. One group of churchmen and women deliberately decided to turn their back on ordinary life, to spend all their time in prayer and worship of God. These were **monks** and **nuns**. **Monasteries** and **nunneries**, where they lived, were set up to allow them to worship undisturbed and were often surrounded by walls or put in remote places to keep the rest of the world away.

The rules that the monks and nuns followed were first set out by Saint Benedict, who lived in Italy in the late 5th and early 6th century. When writing his rules he stated:

We are starting our monastery so that we can study the service of God. We hope the life will not be harsh or too difficult. Instead, our faith will grow and we will follow God's commandments with joy. We will remain in the monastery until we die. As we will share in the sufferings of Christ, we hope to share in his glory in Heaven.

The three most important rules were:

Obedience – to follow God's will through the church leaders.

Poverty – to own nothing.

Chastity – to have nothing to do with the opposite sex, including marrying or having children.

These were the goals of all good clergy, but were meant to be kept very strictly by monks and nuns. To show that they had accepted these rules monks would wear a **habit**, a kind of robe, and have a **tonsure**, whereby the top of the head was shaved. Nuns would also wear habits and keep their hair short, wearing a **wimple**, a kind of hood. Over time a number of different groups, or **orders**, of monks and nuns developed, each trying to follow the Benedictine rules in their own way.

A medieval monk receiving a tonsure; from a manuscript produced around 1220

An example of a medieval nun; from an early 16th century book

Some of the orders that were established in England for both monks and nuns included:

Benedictines, who were known as the 'black monks' because of the colour of their habits. Their monasteries, such as Glastonbury and St. Albans, were some of the wealthiest and most powerful in England.

Cluniacs, who thought that church ceremony was very important, so much so that they spent almost all their time in services and did very little study or manual work.

Carthusians, who were very strict and spent most of their time in individual cells, praying and working.

Cistercians, who were known as 'white monks' from the colour of their habits. They tried to be stricter in following the rules than the Benedictines and built their monasteries (such as Fountains Abbey) far from other people. Some of their monasteries became very wealthy.

When many monasteries had become too wealthy and the monks began to forget the rules, new groups of holy orders were created. These were set up by men called **friars** who, rather than having a monastery as a base, travelled the country preaching and begging. They too ended up with much wealth and property in the end. The best known of the friars were the **Franciscans** ('grey friars') and the **Dominicans** ('black friars'). Women were not allowed to preach, so the female version of each of the orders of friars lived like nuns. In England the most popular female order was the **Poor Clares**, founded in 1215.

When the rules were kept strictly, the daily life of monks and nuns would be very hard. Their life would be centred around prayer, study and work and would follow a pattern like this:

Midnight: The monks wake up for **Matins**, a service of about an hour in the monastery church.

6 am: Wake up again for **Prime**, followed by a breakfast of bread and ale then work or reading.

9 am: **Chapter Mass** in the church and then the monks go to the Chapter House, a place where the rules of the order would be read each day and where monks discussed the running of the monastery.

11 am: **High Mass** in church.

Noon:	Lunch and afternoon nap.
2 pm:	**Nones** in church, then work.
4 pm:	**Vespers** in church, then work.
6 pm:	Supper.
7 pm:	**Compline**, then to bed.

An artist's impression of life in a medieval monastery

In some ways monasteries and nunneries were set up much like a school. There was a place for everyone to meet, a dining-room, kitchens, lavatories, a library and places to work. Monasteries could also provide services for the surrounding villages, even though the monks tried to live separately.

- They were often the only schools for boys to learn to read and write Latin.

- Monasteries kept most of the books that existed and the monks copied them and wrote more.

- Monasteries provided places for travellers to stop and receive shelter.

- Alms (gifts of food, clothing or money) were given to the poor.

- Monasteries could help the sick with medicines.

- As monasteries and nunneries became wealthier they needed more servants, providing jobs for the local people.

Too much wealth for the Church

Wealthy men and women gave money and property to the Church in the hope that this would help them reach Heaven. As the monasteries grew wealthier, sometimes the Benedictine rules were relaxed or forgotten. In time this was to make members of the clergy unpopular with many ordinary people in Europe. But most priests and monks and nuns continued to do their best to worship God in the way they had been taught.

Exercise 3.4

Write out the following paragraph filling in the blanks:

In a medieval village one of the most important buildings would be the _____.
There the villagers would go to listen to the _____ and hear the most
important service, _____. In Britain all the churches belonged to the
_____ _____ Church. Even the days the villagers did not have to work,
known as _____, were set by the Church.

The priest was a very important man in his village. It was he who would _____
the babies, _____ couples and _____ the dead. He might also
_____ the local boys.

Exercise 3.5

Write a sentence or two about each of the following:

1. A diocese

2. Bishops

3. Cathedrals

4. Tithes

5. The Pope

Exercise 3.6

Read the following sources and then answer the questions:

SOURCE A: From a contemporary book about the Rule of St. Benedict.

No monk is allowed private possessions. So the abbot must supply the monks with all they need – habits, socks, shoes, rope belts, a knife, a needle, handkerchiefs and writing instruments.

The abbot must often inspect the monk's beds – to find if they have private possessions hidden there. If anything is found which the abbot has not issued, the monk will be severely punished.

SOURCE B: From *The Canterbury Tales* by Geoffrey Chaucer.

There was a Monk, a leader of the fashions;
Inspecting farms and hunting were his passions...
This Monk was therefore a good man to horse;
Greyhounds he had, as swift as birds, of course.
Hunting a hare, or riding at a fence
Was all his fun, and he spared no expense.
I saw his sleeves were garnished at the hand
With fine grey fur, the finest in the land,
And where his hood was fastened at his chin
He had a wrought-gold, cunningly-made pin...

1. Look at Source A. How did an abbot make sure his monks followed the rule of poverty? When answering make sure you use a quotation from the source.

2. Look at Source B. Give several ways that the writer shows that the monk was not following the rule of poverty. Again, make sure you use quotations in your answer.

3. Look at both sources. How do both help us understand what life was like for monks in the medieval period?

Exercise 3.7

Read the following source and then answer the questions:

SOURCE C: From *The Canterbury Tales* by Geoffrey Chaucer.

> There was also a nun, a prioress,
> Whose smile was simple and coy;
> Her greatest oath was, 'By St. Eloi!'
> And she was known as Madame Eglentyne.
> She sang the divine service very well,
> And nicely intoned through the nose;
> And she spoke French fairly and elegantly
> As she'd been taught at Stratford-at-Bow...
> No question, she had the greatest charm,
> She was so pleasant, and so warm;
> At pains to show to the court
> That she had manners, dignity and reverence;
> But, to speak of her conscience,
> She was so charitable and full of pity
> That she would weep to see
> A mouse caught in a trap...

1. How does Chaucer make it clear that the nun was well-educated?

2. Compare the nun to the monk in Source B on page 45. Which of these two members of the Church do you think most closely followed the rules of the Church? Explain you answer, using quotations.

Exercise 3.8

Under the title 'Life in a monastery or nunnery', make a chart with two headings, *Good* and *Bad*. List what you think are the good and bad points of living as a monk or nun in the correct columns. Which have the most points? Why do you think people became monks and nuns? (Remember what you learned in Chapter 2 about what life was like for ordinary people.)

Chapter 4 From civil war to Henry II

Stephen, 1135-1154

At the death of Henry I in 1135, if the old king's wishes had been respected, his daughter Matilda would have become the next ruler. Instead, Henry's nephew, Stephen, Count of Blois, rushed to England and claimed the crown for himself (see the family tree on page 167). Perhaps not surprisingly, most barons and churchmen supported Stephen's claim. Firstly, he was a man and the country had never been ruled by a woman. Also, the fact that one of the most powerful churchmen, the Bishop of Winchester, was Stephen's brother, obviously helped his cause.

Stephen and civil war

Stephen was in many ways a kind and generous man. One famous story has it that Stephen held hostage a boy named William, whose father had betrayed the king. By all rights Stephen should have had the boy hanged, but instead was found in his tent playing knights with him. The boy was to grow up to be William the Marshal, one of the greatest warrior knights England has ever known. He would make his name in the tournaments held in Europe since the 11th century, and

Stephen, nephew of Henry I; from the manuscript of Piers Langtoft's History of England, produced around 1300

would eventually become the Earl of Pembroke. Unfortunately, a kind king is not always an effective king. Stephen soon faced major problems he could not solve.

Matilda did not simply sit by and hope Stephen would fail. She wanted to defeat the king and so landed in England and raised an army. Thus began a civil war that lasted for fourteen years. So many Englishmen were unhappy with Stephen's rule that Matilda was able to march to London and prepare to be crowned the true ruler of England. But Matilda was proud and full of her own importance and turned the Londoners against her. They actually drove her out of the city. In the end neither side could win full control of England. At different times both Stephen and Matilda were captured by the other side and then escaped or were released.

During the civil war some men took advantage of the chaos to make themselves more powerful. A monk in Peterborough wrote that the barons:

> ...greatly oppressed the wretched people by making them work at their castles... and when the castles were finished they filled them with devils and evil men. Then they took those whom they thought to have any goods, both men and women, and put them in prison for their gold and silver, and tortured them with pains unspeakable.

One man who used the civil war to grow in power was Geoffrey de Mandeville. He changed sides when it suited him and took his soldiers on raids throughout the countryside, burning, stealing and taking prisoners for blackmail. He became the Earl of Essex before being killed in 1144.

When Matilda left England in 1153 the war continued, led by Henry, her son from her second marriage, who was already the Duke of Normandy. Stephen eventually came to an agreement with Henry and, when he died in 1154, it was Henry who became the next king.

Henry II with archbishop Thomas Becket; from the manuscript of Piers Langtoft's History of England, produced around 1300

Henry II, 1154-1189

Henry was twenty-two years old when he became King, and was short and strongly built with a freckled face, red hair and a terrible temper. He was a man of massive energy who found it difficult to stay in one place for very long. It is said that he always had either a bow or a book in his hand, so there is no doubt Henry was very active.

The new King quickly took control of his kingdom. Henry had any illegal castles that had been built during the years of civil war destroyed. Hired foreign soldiers living in the country were forced to leave. He took back the northern part of England from the King of Scotland.

But Henry was not just ruling over England. His marriage to Eleanor of Aquitaine brought him even more lands in France than he had already held from his father. Henry, while a vassal of the King of France, actually held more land in France than anyone else and he was to spend much of his reign there, rather than in England.

A Victorian artist's impression of Eleanor of Aquitaine, queen of France and England, wife of Henry II and mother to Henry, Richard, Geoffrey and John

Eleanor of Aquitaine

In the male-dominated medieval world, Eleanor stands out as a very strong character. She was married at the age of thirteen to the King of France, Louis VII. As she was the heir of her father Duke William X, lord of the county of Poitou and the duchies of Aquitaine and Gascony, she brought to her marriage a huge area of southern France. Eleanor had been brought up in a court full of music and courtly love poetry and did not find her life in northern France comfortable or pleasant. Many of King Louis's supporters were unhappy about her power over the King.

When she was twenty-one, Eleanor insisted on joining Louis as he led the Second Crusade and followed the crusading armies to the Holy Land. As we will learn in Chapter 5, the Crusades were a series of military expeditions launched in the name of the Church to recover the Holy Lands, and Jerusalem in particular, from the Muslims. When Louis's army reached Constantinople, capital of the Byzantine Empire, an eyewitness account stated:

> *Even women travelled in the ranks of the crusaders, dressed as men and armed with lance and battle axe. At the head of these was one in particular, richly-dressed, who, because of the gold embroidery on the hem of her dress, was nicknamed Golden Foot.*

Medieval France and the Angevin holdings

This richly-dressed leader was probably Eleanor. She continued to travel with the crusaders as they marched to Jerusalem and has been accused by some writers of distracting the King. Louis was not a very successful commander and he failed to keep his army under control. Things were made worse when his ally Emperor Conrad's army was all but destroyed by the Turks. Eleanor's own actions – she encouraged one of her barons to ignore King Louis's instructions of where to set up camp – helped lead to a major crusader defeat as the army struggled through the mountains before finally reaching the crusader states.

Crusader states were areas of the Holy Land which were under the control of European princes as a result of previous successes in the Crusades. One of the crusader states, Antioch, was held by Eleanor's uncle, Raymond of Poitiers. Once Louis's army reached Antioch, rumours soon spread that niece and uncle were becoming too close. Certainly, Raymond may have been trying to use the queen in order to convince Louis to help him, rather than push on to Jerusalem. It was also becoming clear that Eleanor was not happy with her husband. This was not helped when Louis had Eleanor seized and carried out of Antioch to rejoin what remained of the crusader army as it made its way to Jerusalem. Soon afterwards the Second Crusade came to an embarrassing end when the French army was defeated outside the walls of Damascus. Louis and Eleanor, with the Queen still in disgrace, made their way slowly home, with Eleanor falling ill several times during the journey.

In 1152, Louis had their marriage annulled by the Church. Within two months, the twenty-six-year-old Eleanor married the nineteen-year-old Henry, who was to become King of England in 1154. King Louis was furious when he found out, for he believed Henry to be his greatest threat.

The King's Justice

Henry wanted to do more than settle the country after the civil war; he wanted to continue the work started by his grandfather, Henry I, to increase royal justice. He encouraged the growth of travelling royal courts, called **assizes**, which took power away from the local baron's court and helped create a common law for all of England. It was also to his advantage that all the fees and fines from the courts now went to the king.

Before the changes made by Henry I, and then Henry II, court cases were often settled by **ordeals**. Ordeal by fire meant that the accused had to pick up a red hot bar of metal and carry it for three paces. The burnt hand was then sealed by a priest and examined after three days. If there was a very large blister it was believed that

God had declared the accused guilty. If the hand was healed, it was believed that he was innocent. The same idea was carried out using boiling water, with the accused having to plunge an arm into the water and pull out a stone from the bottom of the cauldron. Again, when the bandages were removed after three days and the arm was found to be still badly scalded, the person was believed guilty. In some cases, trial by combat could be carried out, the idea being that God would make sure that the guilty party lost in a fight.

Ordeals had been used as a way of conducting a trial for several hundred years. This early source shows the important role the Church played in these cases:

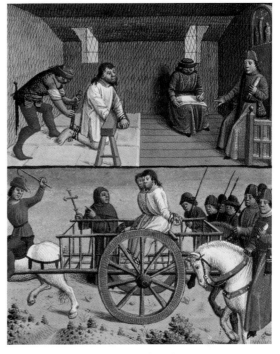

Trial by ordeal; from a medieval manuscript produced around 1375

> Having performed the mass, the priest shall descend to the place appointed, where the trial itself shall be conducted; he shall carry with him the book of the gospels, and a cross… and he shall bless the water before it boils…

> He who puts his hand in the water shall say the Lord's Prayer, and shall sign himself with the sign of the cross, and he shall extract the stone in the name of God himself. Afterwards, his hand shall be bandaged, signed with the seal of the judge, until the third day; when it shall be viewed and judged of by suitable men.

Henry II and Thomas Becket

Henry needed help with the work he was doing with the government and found a strong helper and friend in Thomas Becket. Becket was the son of a Norman merchant and was born in London and educated in the Church. He became Royal Chancellor, making him the King's right-hand man. The two men, tall, dark Becket and short, energetic Henry, became firm friends. Then the old Archbishop of Canterbury died and Henry thought he saw a chance to increase his power. He talked his friend Becket into agreeing to become the new archbishop in 1162, although Becket was not very keen. With his friend as archbishop, Henry believed he would have the chance to make the Church do what he wanted.

But Henry had misjudged Becket, who threw himself into the role of protector of the Church. Very soon the King and he began to quarrel. The argument was about what should be done with criminous clerks, that is, churchmen who had committed a crime. At this time, these men were not tried in the king's courts, but in Church courts, which did not punish them as harshly, and many thought this was unfair. This also meant the fines and fees went to the Church, not the king. But the dispute was more than just about the court system. It was the same kind of argument that William II had had with Archbishop Anselm. The real question was, who was really in charge in England: the king or the Church?

The quarrel between Henry II and Thomas Becket was in many ways about two stubborn men, neither of whom would give in. In 1164 Henry tried to force Becket to agree to a set of rules called the Constitutions of Clarendon, which stated that no king's man could be **excommunicated** (not allowed to be part of the Church and its services) without the king's permission; that no churchman could leave the country without the king's permission; and that criminous clerks would be tried in Church courts, but if found guilty would be sentenced by the king's court. When Becket proved unwilling to accept these rules, Henry tried to put him on trial for mishandling money when he had been the Royal Chancellor. Becket decided to go into exile in France, where he stayed at a monastery at Pontigny. The outraged King seized his lands and property. For the next five years neither man was ready to give in. Perhaps Henry was bitter because he felt that his old friend had betrayed him.

It was Henry's problems with his sons that helped bring his trouble with Becket to a head. Henry's oldest living son, Prince Henry, was impatient to have more power. Because he held so much land in France which needed his attention, King Henry decided to make his son King of England, but still under his control. To do this a **coronation** ceremony was needed, in which the head of the Church in England would place the crown on the new king's head. The problem was that, while this should have been Archbishop Becket, Henry II instead turned to the other English Archbishop, Roger of York. Unfortunately for King Henry, this proved one step too far for the Pope and the Church. The outcry forced Henry to meet Becket in France to try to patch up their differences. The two old friends seemed to make up and Becket was allowed to return to England in December 1170.

As soon as he was back in Canterbury, however, Becket showed that all had not been forgotten or forgiven. He announced that all the bishops that had taken part in Prince Henry's coronation were excommunicated, and he complained to the Pope about Roger. The bishops and Archbishop Roger quickly made their way to Henry II's court in France. They told Henry about this and said that Becket was misusing his powers. In a rage the King was reported to have cried out 'Will no one rid me of this turbulent priest?' Four knights, Reginald Fitzurse, Hugh de Morville, William de Tracy and Richard le Breton, heard this and believed it was their chance to impress the King. In the next few days they sailed over to England and made their way to Canterbury.

They were joined by members of the de Broc family, who hated Becket because they had been given his lands by Henry, only for Becket to take them back after making peace with the King. On 29th December 1170 they arrived at Becket's palace next to the cathedral and marched in to arrest him. Meanwhile Henry, realising what was happening, had sent a messenger to stop the knights, but he was to arrive far too late.

Thomas Becket met the four knights, who tried to argue with him about his actions, but the clever archbishop quickly made them look and sound foolish. The knights stormed off outside to put on their armour and arm themselves. Becket's servants and clergymen saw that trouble was coming and locked the door of the palace. They then talked Becket into going to the cathedral for the next religious service and virtually carried the reluctant Archbishop through an underground passage to his church. Meanwhile, the knights had returned to the palace to find their way blocked, then found another way in and discovered that Becket was gone. The knights and their followers went in search of the missing archbishop.

Becket and his clergymen in the cathedral prepared themselves for the service. When some of the monks attempted to lock the cathedral doors Becket stopped them, declaring that his church was not a castle. As the service began a door opened with a bang and one of the knights demanded in a loud voice, 'Where is Thomas Becket, traitor to King and country?' The Archbishop called out in reply 'Here I am, no traitor but a priest of God.' After more angry words the knights tried to carry Becket out of the cathedral, which seems to have led to

The death of Archbishop Thomas Becket; from a 15th century manuscript

pushing and shoving between the Archbishop and his attackers. It may be then that Becket realised that things had gone too far, for he knelt down to pray and the knights drew their swords. One struck the Archbishop so hard on his head that the top of it came off and the sword struck the floor of the cathedral and shattered. One of the knights' followers stuck his sword into Becket's skull, spreading the blood and brains, and called out, 'That fellow will not rise again.' After killing Becket, the knights went through his palace, stealing what they wanted, and rode off.

Becket's death was a disaster for Henry II. His attempts to control the Church had to be given up and criminous clerks continued to be tried in church courts. He was blamed by many for the murder of the Archbishop and he does seem to have been very upset by the death of his old friend. In 1174 Henry II walked through the city of Canterbury barefoot and in simple robes and allowed churchmen to whip him as penance, showing his sorrow and asking forgiveness for the murder. As for the knights who had carried out the murder, their penance was to be ordered to go on crusade.

Henry II and his family

Henry's final years were not to be happy. He had fallen out with his wife, Eleanor, but only after she had produced a number of children, including four sons, Henry, Richard, Geoffrey, and John. Eleanor has often either been ignored by historians as merely a queen, having no real power, or been seen as a troublemaker and untrustworthy. The truth is that she was instrumental for years in helping Henry hold together his vast empire. Nearly always travelling, Henry often left Eleanor to keep a watchful eye on parts of his kingdom, such as England, particularly during the period when Henry was in conflict with Archbishop Becket. Eleanor also travelled to her lands in the south of France to try to help her husband control his troublesome barons there. In 1168, she decided to live apart from Henry, perhaps because of the many affairs he was involved in with other women, or maybe because she was now 48 and beyond the age that she could safely produce children. What is clear is that, by 1172, Eleanor was ready to turn against her husband in support of her sons.

The young princes were eager for more power and gave Henry a great deal of trouble. Spoilt by their father, they were impatient for real power and jealous of each other. King Louis of France was eager to take advantage of this situation and Eleanor wanted justice for her sons and perhaps more influence and authority for herself. The result was a dangerous revolt against Henry that was eventually also to include the King of Scotland. Henry, having been forewarned, had Eleanor captured as she tried to make her way to Poitiers. The Queen was to be kept a prisoner for the next decade.

Meanwhile his sons Henry, Richard and Geoffrey rose up in rebellion along with a number of the King's vassals. For two years, 1173-1174, Henry spent his time rushing from one part of his empire to another to beat back various attacks. Success finally came when the King of Scotland was defeated and captured. Henry received the news on the evening of the day he had paid penance in front of Becket's tomb. There were many, including Henry, who believed that he had been forgiven by God and Becket. 'God be thanked for it and St. Thomas the Martyr,' said the King.

Although two of his sons, Henry and Geoffrey, died before their father (see the family tree on page 167), Richard rebelled again in 1188 and even the youngest son, Henry's favourite, John, was involved. They were aided by the young King of France, Philip II. Together they defeated the ageing King, who was said to have died of a broken heart in his castle at Chinon in France in 1189.

Exercise 4.1
Match the following halves of sentences together correctly:

1.	Matilda	(a) was one of the great warrior knights.
2.	William the Marshal	(b) became king after Henry I.
3.	Londoners	(c) was the daughter of Henry I.
4.	Stephen of Blois	(d) forced Matilda to leave their city.
5.	Henry II	(e) was the son of Matilda.

Exercise 4.2
Write a sentence or two about each of the following:

1. Geoffrey de Mandeville

2. Eleanor of Aquitaine

3. Assizes

4. The de Broc family

5. Criminous clerks

Exercise 4.3

Look at pages 51-54 and read about the quarrel between Thomas Becket and Henry II.

1. Make a list of the reasons why Becket and the King argued.

2. Now rewrite your list, putting at the top the most important reason for the quarrel.

3. Why did you choose the reason at the top?

Exercise 4.4

Read the following account, written by Edward Grim, a monk who was an eyewitness to the murder of Thomas Becket. Answer the questions that follow.

> Then the unconquered martyr, seeing the hour at hand which should put an end to this miserable life... inclined his neck as one who prays and, joining his hands, he lifted them up... The wicked knight, fearing lest he should be rescued by the people and escape alive, leapt upon him suddenly and wounded this lamb on the head, cutting off the top of the crown and by the same blow he wounded the arm of him who tells this. Then Archbishop Becket received a second blow on the head but still stood firm. At the third blow he fell on his knees and elbows, offering himself a living victim and saying in a low voice, "For the Name of Jesus and the protection of the Church I am ready to embrace death." Then the third knight inflicted a terrible wound as he lay, by which the sword was broken against the pavement, and the crown was separated from the head.

1. Write down two ways in which the writer describes Archbishop Becket.

2. Find an example of how the writer feels about the knights.

3. What happened to the writer during the attack on Becket?

4. How many times was Becket struck before he died?

5. Compare Edward Grim's account to the picture of the death of Archbishop Becket on page 53. Do they agree or disagree? Explain your answer. Make sure to state clearly what the picture shows and then compare it to Grim's account, using quotations when possible.

Exercise 4.5

Write the story of the quarrel between Thomas Becket and Henry II. Start with a short paragraph explaining the background and how the two met. Your paragraphs could start with these sentences:

- 'Thomas Becket served Henry II well in government.'

- 'Henry II's mistake was to convince Becket to become Archbishop of Canterbury.'

- 'The quarrel between the two men became serious when...'

- 'Making peace in 1170 did not work.'

Finish with a concluding paragraph looking at what the death of Becket meant to the Church and to Henry II.

Chapter 5 Richard I, the Crusades and King John

Richard I, the 'Lionheart', 1189-1199

Richard I was known as 'Lionheart' because of his bravery and because of a story that he had once faced a lion and killed it by reaching down its throat and pulling out its heart. He was a very tall and physically powerful man for the time, perhaps standing nearly two metres in height. A writer of the time, Richard de Templo, said he was:

> ...graceful in figure; his hair between red and auburn; his limbs were straight and flexible, his arms rather long and not to be matched for wielding a sword, and his long legs suited the rest of his frame, while his appearance was commanding.

During his reign, Richard spent only six months in total in England. Where was he the rest of the time, and what was he doing? To understand this means going back in time and looking at the story of the Crusades.

The First Crusade

The Crusades were a series of military campaigns launched in the name of the Church to recover the Holy Land from the Muslims. The Holy Land is an area in the

Middle East containing modern-day Israel (Palestine), Lebanon, Jordan and Syria. In the Middle Ages, this was an important place for three major religions: Judaism, Christianity and Islam.

The crusades were started for a number of reasons. A strong belief in Christianity and support for the Roman Catholic Church were very important, as men who decided to go on crusade would leave everything behind, run up debts, and face sickness and death in a strange land. But it was felt that control of the Holy Land by the Muslims was a threat to all Christians, and to go on crusade counted as a holy pilgrimage, ensuring one's soul would not go to Hell.

Richard I, known as the Lionheart, and son of Henry II; from the manuscript of Historia Anglorum by Matthew Paris, produced around 1255

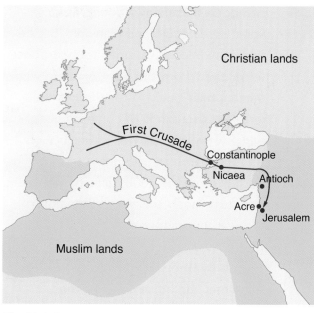

The Holy Land and the First Crusade

The leaders of the Byzantine Empire had also asked Western Europe for help. Surviving after the fall of Rome in 476AD, the Byzantine Empire had controlled much of the Middle East and Turkey, but was under great pressure from Turkish Muslim invaders.

The men who would 'take the cross' and go on crusade lived in a violent age and were used to settling their differences using the force of arms. When the call for a crusade came, Pope Urban II made a stirring speech encouraging Christians to fight. Archbishop Balderic of Dol reported what the Pope had said:

> *You oppressors of orphans, you robbers of widows, you murderers... you robbers of others' rights... if you want to take counsel for your souls you must either cast off as quickly as possible the belt of this sort of knighthood or go forward boldly as knights of Christ, hurrying swiftly to defend the Eastern Church.*

What better way for violent men to reach Heaven than to use their military skills for the glory of the Church? So, in a field at Clermont in France in November 1095, Pope Urban II announced the launch of the First Crusade, with its main target the city of Jerusalem.

This is how the event was recorded in the *Gesta Francorum*, an account of the crusades written around 1100 by an unknown writer who travelled to the Holy Land with Bohemund of Antioch, one of the leaders of the First Crusade:

> *Pope Urban with his archbishops, bishops, abbots, and priests, set out as quickly as possible beyond the mountains and began to deliver sermons and to preach, saying: "Whoever wishes to save his soul should not hesitate humbly to take up the way of the Lord, and if he lacks sufficient money, divine mercy will give him enough."*

Pope Urban II launching the First Crusade; from a manuscript produced around 1490

He hoped that many a young, fit knight would agree to go and many did. But he did not expect the tremendous response he received from the poor, many of whom joined a man called Peter the Hermit. Peter led thousands of common people, men and women, as well as knights, on the long march to the Holy Land, a journey of nearly 2000 miles to Jerusalem. Not surprisingly there was little control of these thousands and there was major trouble as they marched through Hungary and the Byzantine Empire. When they finally met the Muslim forces, the undisciplined army was slaughtered, although Peter escaped.

Meanwhile, another army was forming, with knights coming from all across Western Europe, including William I's son-in-law Stephen of Blois and his son Robert of Normandy. Altogether, this second wave of the First Crusade may have numbered up to 50 000 strong and they all began to make their way to the Holy Land, most over land, some by sea. After meeting at the Byzantine Empire's capital of Constantinople, the crusaders took the city of Nicaea with Byzantine help and began to march south. When the Muslim forces attacked them at Dorylaeum, the crusaders managed to defeat them. But the crusaders were nearly destroyed by their march across Asia Minor, from both the harsh conditions (lack of food and water) and the arguments amongst their leaders.

The siege of Antioch

When the army came to Antioch, it settled down to besiege the city, but by Christmas 1097 the crusaders were starving. When a Muslim army appeared at Antioch, only 700 crusader knights still had a horse to ride. And although this small force managed to beat off the enemy, many of the crusaders began to desert, including Peter the Hermit himself, who escaped before being dragged reluctantly back to camp.

Antioch was taken in the end with help from the largely Christian population inside the walls, but was then immediately placed under siege by a new, large Muslim army. A Muslim historian named Ibn Al-Athir, who wrote at the same time and may even have witnessed the events himself, gives the following account. Although the crusaders were made up of knights from many Western countries, some historians of the time tended to refer to them as 'Franks', meaning people from what is now France:

> After taking Antioch the Franks [i.e. Christians] *camped there for twelve days without* *food. The wealthy ate their horses and the poor ate rotten meat and leaves from the* *trees. Faced with this situation, their leaders wrote to Kerbuqa* [a Turkish leader] *to ask* *for safe passage through his territory but he refused, saying "You will have to fight your* *way out".*

When, in desperation, the starving crusaders marched out to attack the besiegers, to their amazement the Muslim army fell apart, for they argued amongst themselves as much as the crusaders did. As Ibn Al-Athir reported:

> [The Christians] *left the city in groups of five or six. The Muslims said to Kerbuqa:* *"You should go up to the city and kill them one by one as they come out; it is easy to* *pick them off now that they have split up." He replied: "No, wait until they have all* *come out and then we will kill them." He would not allow them to attack the enemy,* *and when some Muslims killed a group of Franks, he went himself to stop it from* *happening again. When all the Franks had come out they began to attack strongly, and* *the Muslims turned and fled. This was Kerbuqa's fault, firstly because he had treated his* *own men with such contempt and scorn, and secondly because he had prevented them* *from killing the Franks. The Muslims were completely defeated without striking a single* *blow or firing a single arrow.*

The siege of Jerusalem

In January 1099, the crusaders began their march south again, through Syria and Palestine. There was little fighting, as the local Muslim leaders feared the crusaders' ruthlessness and let them march through unhindered. On 7th June the crusaders first caught sight of the walls of Jerusalem. The remaining army, only 1500 strong, laid siege to the city and help soon arrived with the arrival of Genoese and English ships with materials to build siege engines. On 15th July, with the help of a giant siege tower, the crusaders managed to breach the walls. They charged into the city and rushed to open the gates. Thousands of crusaders poured into Jerusalem and proceeded to slaughter all the Muslims and Jews they could find. After nearly four years, the prize for which they had been striving was finally in their hands. Ibn Al-Athir wrote:

The Franks moved on to Jerusalem and beseiged it for more than six weeks. They built two towers, one of which, near Sion, the Muslims burnt down, killing everyone inside it. It had barely stopped burning when a messenger arrived, bringing the news that the other side of the city had fallen, and asking for help. Jerusalem was taken from the north on the morning of Friday 15th July 1099.

The capture and looting of Jerusalem by the crusaders; from a manuscript produced around 1440 by the artist Jean de Courcy

The crusader states

With much of the Holy Land now in Christian hands, the crusaders divided it into different crusader states. The intention was that these states would be ruled by Christian leaders on behalf of the Church. But of course the Muslims who lived there had other ideas, and it was soon apparent that a permanent army of occupation would be required to keep the Holy Lands in Christian hands.

Certainly some of the knights who went on crusade were prepared to stay. There is evidence that some took their wives with them, and raised families in the crusader states. It was not unknown for some Christian women to respond to the Pope's call by fighting in the army alongside the men. This greatly surprised the Muslim fighters, as a contemporary writer called Baha Ad-Din relates:

> *An observant old soldier who entered the trenches that day told me that on the other side of the wall was a woman dressed in a green mantle, who shot at us with a wooden bow and wounded many Muslims before she was killed.*

A few of the crusaders who stayed even took on some of the Muslim customs. Usama ibn Mungidh (1095-1188) wrote of an encounter his friend had with a retired crusader knight:

> *We came to the house of one of the old knights who came with the First Crusade. This man had retired from the army, and was living on the income of the property he owned in Antioch. He had a fine table brought out, spread with a splendid selection of appetising food. He saw that I was not eating, and said: "Don't worry, please; eat what you like, for I don't eat Frankish food. I have Egyptian cooks and eat only what they serve. No pig's flesh ever comes into my house!" So I ate.*

But many soon left for home, and when a new wave of crusaders tried to march to the Holy Land, most died or turned back whilst crossing Asia Minor. The unlucky Stephen of Blois, who had deserted before reaching Jerusalem, returned, only to die in battle trying to stop a Muslim army re-taking Palestine.

The Christian kingdom of Jerusalem had been founded, but its hold on the Holy Land was to prove weak. The Second Crusade, led by Louis VII of France, set out to reinforce Jersulam, but ended in failure after a short and ineffective siege of Damascus in 1148.

The Third Crusade

Although they had been defeated and forced to give up control of their lands, the Muslims soon began to fight back more effectively. In 1187, under the leadership of Saladin, Muslim forces began to recapture much of the Holy Land. The fighting was intense, and severe. The Muslims had not forgotten the treatment their ancestors had suffered when the crusaders captured Jerusalem many years before, as the historian Ibn Al-Athir relates:

> *When the Franks saw how violently the Muslims were attacking, how continuous and effective was the fire from the ballistas and how busily the sappers were breaching the walls, meeting no resistance, they grew desperate and their leaders gathered together for advice. They decided to ask for safe-conduct out of the city and to hand Jerusalem over to Saladin. They sent a group of their lords and nobles to ask for terms, but*

Saladin refused to grant their request. "We shall deal with you," he said, "just as you dealt with the population of Jerusalem when you took it in 1099, with murder and enslavement and other such savageries!"

Jerusalem did fall, as did many other crusader-held towns and castles.

In response the Pope called for another crusade to 'save' the Holy Land for Christianity. (The Roman Catholic Church at this time did not believe in tolerating other religions.) In 1191, Richard I and King Philip II of France both agreed to 'take up the cross' and join this crusade. Richard chose to travel by sea to reach the Holy Land after raising as much money as possible. Richard landed at Cyprus in May and seized it, creating a crusader base that was to last for centuries to come. He also decided to marry the daughter of the King of Navarre, Berengaria, instead of the sister of King Philip, to whom he had been engaged for twenty years.

The fall of Acre

When Richard and his army finally arrived in the Holy Land, they found a crusader army surrounding the city of Acre, but another Muslim army under Saladin surrounding the crusaders. The crusaders were the survivors of the earlier defeats in the Holy Land, together with King Philip's army and the remainders of a German army whose leader had drowned on the march. When not fighting the Muslims they were busy quarrelling amongst themselves.

Richard the Lionheart on crusade; from a 19th century children's history book

With Richard's arrival, Saladin's army was kept at bay, the siege was tightened and the fleet was used to make sure no supplies could reach the defenders of Acre. We know this from the account of Baha Ad-Din, who said: 'The Franks had posted their ships all round Acre to blockade the harbour against Muslim shipping. The beseiged were in dire need of food and provisions.' Both Richard and King Philip fell sick, but this did not stop Richard from being carried out on a litter to encourage his men in the fighting. In July 1191, the city surrendered to the crusaders and a truce with Saladin was agreed. As the crusaders crowded into the city, the leader of the Germans, Duke Leopold of Austria, had his banner placed on the walls along with those of the kings of France and England, despite his having played no part in the fighting. In anger the English threw the banner off the walls, something Leopold was not to forget.

The fall of Acre; from a 15th century manuscript

With the fall of Acre, King Philip of France, who was ill, decided to return home, leaving Richard more or less in charge of the crusade. Saladin, however, was not to give up so easily. And his determination to defeat Richard in battle must have been increased when Richard, feeling that Saladin was not carrying out his agreement concerning the surrender of Acre, had several thousand Muslim captives massacred in full view of Saladin's army. According to the chronicle of Baha Ad-Din:

> When the English King saw that Saladin delayed in carrying out the terms of the treaty, he broke his word to the Muslim prisoners... On the afternoon of 20th August he and all the Frankish army rode to the wells below Tall al-'Ayadiyya... They brought up the Muslim prisoners, more than three thousand men in chains. They fell on them as one man and slaughtered them in cold blood, with sword and lance... The next morning the Muslims found their companions lying where they fell, and some they recognized. Great grief seized them, and from then on they did not spare any enemy prisoners, except for well-known persons and strong men who could be put to work.

Jaffa and Jerusalem

In August the crusaders marched on Jaffa, 70 miles to the south of Acre. Saladin's army also moved and intercepted Richard's army at Arsuf the following month. Richard proved to be a brilliant general, however, understanding how to use his army to its best advantage and driving the Muslims back, although at one point the battle was almost lost when his knights charged without orders.

Jaffa was quickly taken and its defences repaired while the crusaders prepared for an attack on Jerusalem. But then everything started to go wrong. When Richard's army marched to Jerusalem, the weather was so bad that they had to pull back. Arguments began about who should rule the crusader states in the Holy Land and even who should control Acre. These disputes were settled and Richard took one of Saladin's fortresses at Darum, but Jerusalem was still just out of reach. Richard had been on crusade for over two years and reports were beginning to reach him of trouble in England, and of King Philip's plans to attack his lands in France.

Once again the crusaders marched on Jerusalem and once again they came close enough to see the city, but were again forced to turn back. The story goes that Richard covered his eyes with his shield and, in tears, said he would not look upon Jerusalem if he could not free it from the Muslims.

Then Saladin struck. With Richard's army intent on taking Jerusalem, the Muslims launched an attack on Jaffa. Hearing this, Richard arrived by ship and waded ashore, leading a small band of men. He caught the Muslim attackers, who were busy plundering the town, by surprise and drove them from the city. Richard continued to try to work out a truce with Saladin and, when the Muslims once again tried a quick attack on Jaffa, Richard proved his worth as a warrior king, once more defeating Saladin's forces. But Richard was sick, his troops were tired

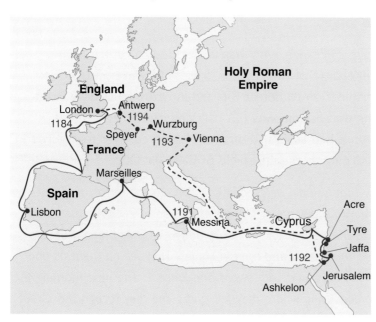

Richard I and the route of the Third Crusade

and the King wanted to return to his lands in England and France. Saladin sent fruit to the ill King, along with snow to cool Richard's drinks. He promised that the crusaders could keep all the towns they had conquered down to Jaffa and that Christian pilgrims could visit the holy places unharmed, but he insisted crusader holdings further south than Jaffa had to be surrendered. Finally Richard agreed; his role in the Third Crusade was over.

Richard's captivity

When Richard set sail from the Holy Land in October 1192, he believed he would reach his kingdom fairly soon. But Richard did not like sea travel, so instead of sailing all the way back to England, he first hired a pirate ship to take him to Italy, then tried to travel through Austria and Germany. Unfortunately the story that the King of England was travelling in disguise spread widely and the King, with two companions, was captured near Vienna that December. The really bad news for Richard was that the man who caught him was Leopold of Austria, whom Richard's men had insulted when they tore down his banner on the walls of Acre.

Richard's problem was that there were a great many people who wanted to see him imprisoned. The Emperor of Germany took control of him and demanded over 100 000 marks for his release. King Philip of France was willing to pay this and more to keep Richard locked up, while he plotted with Richard's brother Prince John to seize Normandy. When in 1194 the money was eventually raised and Richard was released, Philip sent a message to Prince John saying 'the Devil is now loose!'

The death of Richard I

Richard returned to a nearly bankrupt England and found his kingdom in disarray. He swiftly crushed an attempted rebellion led by his brother John, and crossed the Channel to turn his anger on Philip. For the next four years, Richard stayed in France and, with valuable assistance from his mother Eleanor, recovered almost all the lands and castles lost while he had been on crusade and imprisoned. Then, in 1199, Richard was killed. He was attacking a castle at Châlus held by rebel barons when he carelessly came too close to the walls. He did not have his armour on, and was hit by a crossbow bolt in his left shoulder. Because Richard had become fat it was not possible to remove the bolt properly and the wound became infected. As he lay dying, the King decreed that his brother John would rule England next, as he had no children of his own, and forgave the man who had killed him. This seems to have been forgotten, as when the castle was eventually captured, all the soldiers guarding it were hanged by Richard's men except the crossbowman, who was skinned alive.

Richard I was one of the best military leaders ever to be King of England. However, on his death, England was left nearly bankrupt from taxes for the crusades and for his ransom. How would the next king, John, deal with this?

Exercise 5.1

Match the following events with their dates and write them out in chronological (time) order:

1.	Richard is captured by Leopold of Austria.	(a) September 1191
2.	Richard rebels against his father Henry II.	(b) July 1191
3.	Cyprus falls to Richard's soldiers.	(c) 1187
4.	Philip II and Richard lead a successful attack on Acre.	(d) 1189
5.	Richard is crowned and decides to go on crusade.	(e) 1188
6.	The Battle of Arsuf.	(f) December 1192
7.	Richard dies attacking the castle of Châlus.	(g) May 1191
8.	The Pope calls for the Third Crusade.	(h) 1199

Exercise 5.2

Write a sentence or two about each of the following:

1. Prince John

2. Leopold of Austria

3. Princess Berengaria

4. Philip II

5. Saladin

Exercise 5.3

Read the sources and answer the questions that follow:

SOURCE A: From the chronicle of Imad Ad-Din, a Muslim follower of Saladin during the Third Crusade:

> God's will prevailed, and the King of England's request for peace was granted. I helped to draw up the treaty and wrote the text, fixing the boundaries and specifying the

terms, and this was Tuesday 1st September 1192... They agreed a general truce by land and sea, plains and mountains, deserts and cities... The Franks, even when abandoning land formerly held by them, appeared happy and content, and included Tripoli and Antioch in the terms, and the near and distant provinces.

SOURCE B: From *The Crusades*, by Antony Bridge, published in 1980:

When Saladin offered the same terms as those proposed before the battle outside Jaffa, Richard could not afford another long period of haggling, and on 2nd September he signed a treaty of peace which was to last five years...

1. How do these sources differ in their accounts of the truce between Richard and Saladin?

2. Which of the sources do you think is more useful in getting a good idea of the events of the Third Crusade? When explaining your answer, don't forget to look at who produced each source, when it was produced and what it says.

Exercise 5.4

Write out a brief story of Richard I, using the chronological list from Exercise 5.1 to help you. Start with an introduction about his appearance, then outline several of the most important events in his life. Finish with a sentence saying if you think he was a hero and why, based on what you have written in the main part of your story.

Exercise 5.5

1. Look back at page 35 on what made a good king. Make two lists, one headed 'Richard as a good king', one 'Richard as a bad king'. Go through the chapter again and try to find points to put into each list. Overall, how does Richard rate as a king?

2. Now turn this into an essay of four paragraphs with the title 'Was Richard I a good king?' Unlike the story being asked for in Exercise 5.4, this is a chance for you to show more judgement about Richard I. After an introduction stating the question and how you intend to answer it, write one paragraph about Richard the good king. The next paragraph should be on Richard the bad king. Finally, write a paragraph stating whether you think overall Richard was a good or bad king.

King John, brother of Richard I and youngest son of Henry II; from the manuscript of Piers Langtoft's History of England, produced around 1300

John, 1199-1216

Textbooks, films and the Robin Hood stories all agree: King John was 'bad'. Monks writing at the time were more than happy to list John's crimes, which included greed, treachery and murder. From this we should no doubt conclude that John must have been the 'worst' king England ever had. But was he?

John and the Angevin empire

John became King in 1199 with the death of his older brother Richard. Born in 1166, he was short like his father Henry II and was called 'Lackland' because he was the youngest son and at first there were no lands for him to inherit. He has been accused of breaking his father's heart by joining his brother Richard's rebellion against him, and then whilst Richard was on crusade and imprisoned, John does seem to have plotted with King Philip II of France to seize Richard's lands. Clearly he did not wish to remain 'Lackland' for ever. As it turned out and, despite John's previous treachery, Richard forgave his younger brother and made sure that he would follow him as king.

Like the rest of his family, John was more French than he was English. His everyday language was French and he spent a great deal of his early life in the parts of France held by his family. In fact, the English kings at this time controlled more of France than the King of France did himself.

Understandably, the kings of France did not like this situation and Philip II was no exception. As soon as possible, Philip attacked John by claiming that John's

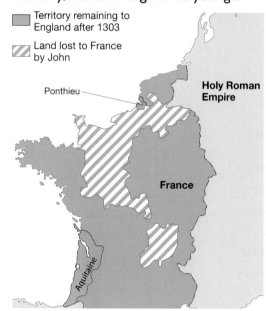

Territory remaining to England after 1303

Land lost to France by John

Ponthieu

Holy Roman Empire

France

Aquitaine

King John's holdings in France

nephew, Arthur, son of his dead brother Geoffrey, had a better claim to the Angevin lands than John did (see map). John was quick to defeat Philip's attack and even managed to capture Arthur. Far from being a 'bad' king, John seemed to be in complete control.

In 1200, John managed to upset an important French baron family, the Lusignans, by marrying Isabella of Angoulême. She was to have married Hugh Lusignan but John, eager to control the land that she was to inherit, divorced his own wife and married the twelve-year-old Isabella.

The tomb of Isabella of Angoulême, second wife of King John, in Fontevrault Abbey

At first, the Lusignan family accepted the change as John arranged another suitable marriage for them, but then they decided to complain to King Philip. Philip demanded that John come before him to explain his actions. John refused and this gave Philip an excuse to attack John's lands in France.

John's position grew difficult. In 1203 there were rumours that he had murdered his captive nephew Arthur. On top of this, John's mother, Eleanor, who was greatly respected by many in both France and England, died on 1st April 1204 at the age of 82. Following her death, many of John's French barons refused to support him. King Philip managed to seize Normandy in 1204 and, soon afterwards, most of the rest of John's French lands were lost.

King John worked hard to build up the money to retake his lost French lands. He made use of a war tax called **scutage**, even when he was not at war and, when his barons were found guilty in the royal courts, they were fined very heavily. And soon he found an even better way of raising money.

John and the Church

In 1198, a new Pope had been elected in Rome and took the title of Innocent III. This Pope was determined to increase the power of the Church, and was prepared to quarrel with anyone to achieve his aim.

Pope Innocent III; from a fresco (wall painting) produced around 1219 at Sacro Speco in Subiaco, Italy

In 1205, the old Archbishop of Canterbury had died and John, like his father Henry II before him, believed he should choose the next archbishop. Innocent III, however, declared that the English scholar Stephen Langton should be the new Archbishop of Canterbury. When John refused to accept Langton, the Pope took action in 1208 by placing an **interdict** on England. This meant that ordinary church services, marriages and burials could not be held. This was a very serious disruption in an age when church services played such an important part in daily life. But for John, it was less serious. While there was no recognised Archbishop of Canterbury, the money that would have gone to the archbishop came instead into the King's own treasury. In 1209, the Pope went further and excommunicated John, but still the King collected Church money and would not give in.

Matthew Paris, a monk at the Abbey of St. Albans, wrote of these times in his chronicle *The deeds of the abbots of St. Albans*:

> *King John instructed the abbot to celebrate divine service during the interdict in spite of the Pope's ban. Having taken advice about this in the chapter, the abbot said: "Brothers, one should obey God rather than man: we shall have to put up with the prince's anger." The King, violently angry at this disobedience of his commands and gladly accepting this excuse for doing injury, took the whole abbey into his hands.*

The Abbot of St. Albans had to pay King John 600 marks, or £400, before he would return the abbey to the Abbot's control.

In 1213, however, John changed his mind about the argument because Innocent III began encouraging Philip II to invade England. John was not yet ready to take on Philip, so he decided that he needed to give in to the Pope's demands. He accepted Stephen Langton as Archbishop, and offered his kingdom to the Pope, making himself Innocent III's vassal. When the Pope accepted, John had managed to turn a deadly enemy into a friend.

How do we know about King John?

John's argument with the Pope helps to explain one reason why he is known as 'bad' King John. During this time in the Middle Ages nearly all the writing was done by monks, who recorded the events of the time in chronicles. One of the best known of these monks was Matthew Paris who wrote around 1250. He continued the work of an earlier monk at the same abbey, Roger of Wendover. Neither man liked John, as the following shows:

> *John lost Normandy and many other lands because of his own laziness. He always took money from his people and destroyed their property.*

The problem with information like this is that many monks made no effort to be balanced and were ready to repeat rumours and stories without checking to see if they were true. For example, Roger of Wendover wrote about the death at John's orders of a priest named Geoffrey, even though documents of the time prove that the 'murdered' man was still alive ten years after John's death (See Source B on page 77). But while this means that at least some of the accounts are not trustworthy or reliable about certain details, they do give a useful idea about how the Church at that time viewed King John.

War and the Magna Carta

By 1214, John felt he was ready to take his French lands back from Philip II. He had made peace with the Pope and an alliance with another powerful monarch in Europe, Otto IV of Germany. Together they planned that, while John was to attack the King of France from the south of France, Otto was to attack in the north. Unfortunately, at the Battle of Bouvines that year, Philip won an unexpected victory against Otto IV and John was forced to agree to a truce with him.

John's English barons had put up with high taxes, unfair treatment in the royal courts and rumours of John's misdeeds. John's failure to win in France was the final straw. They demanded to meet with the King and, when John refused, a number of barons raised an army and, in May 1215, marched to London. John was in no position to fight his barons, so he was forced to meet with them in June at Runnymede, near Windsor Castle. With Archbishop Langton working to bring the two sides together, the barons presented a great charter to John. Reluctantly, King John had to agree to their demands.

The **Magna Carta** is often seen as a key moment in the growth of the rights of the English people. Actually, rather than serving to protect the people, its main purpose was to restrict the King's powers in favour of the barons. Many of the 63 separate statements, or clauses, dealt with immediate complaints of the time, such as John's French friends. However, several clauses had a wider meaning:

- John was instructed to leave the Church alone.

- He was told he could not raise taxes without the consent of his barons.

- The level at which the king could set certain feudal fees such as relief, an inheritance tax, was restricted.

- Freemen could not be imprisoned or punished without a fair trial.

- Freemen could not be fined without trial and any fine they were given should match the crime.

Artist's impression of John adding his seal to the Magna Carta; from a children's history book published in 1905

These clauses were intended to protect the barons, rather than the ordinary people, but you can see why they came to be seen later as important steps towards freedom for all people. However, although the Magna Carta was intended to restore some of the barons' powers which the barons felt that John and his father had taken from them, John had no intention of being bound by it.

As soon as he could, John gathered troops and loyal barons to punish the rebels. His cause was helped when Innocent III declared that John was not bound by the Magna Carta. Civil war broke out in England.

The rebel barons felt that the time was right to rid England of its king, and called upon Philip II of France for help. In May 1216, Philip sent his son Prince Louis, whom the rebels declared to be the rightful king. At first, John did have some military success. He took Rochester Castle and captured a number of rebels, and Dover Castle stubbornly refused to fall to the French. However, the tide was turning against him, and his miseries increased when, while crossing the Wash in East Anglia, he lost a great deal of his baggage including, some stories claim, much of his treasure. Suffering from dysentery, a disease of the intestines very common for soldiers on campaign, and as a result, according to some accounts, of eating too many peaches and drinking too much cider, John died in October 1216.

Exercise 5.6

Match the following events with their dates and write them out in chronological order.

1.	King John dies of dysentery.	(a)	1215
2.	King Philip II takes Normandy from John.	(b)	May 1216
3.	King John becomes a vassal of Pope Innocent III.	(c)	1204
4.	King John is excommunicated by the Pope.	(d)	1208
5.	John agrees to the Magna Carta.	(e)	October 1216
6.	Innocent III places England under an interdict.	(f)	1214
7.	A French army under Prince Louis invades England.	(g)	1209
8.	Otto IV loses the Battle of Bouvines.	(h)	1213

Exercise 5.7

Write a sentence or two about the following:

1. The Angevin Empire

2. Arthur, son of Geoffrey

3. Scutage

4. Interdict

5. Prince Louis

Exercise 5.8

Draw up a table under the title 'What the Magna Carta said', with three columns headed: 'Religion', 'Taxes' and 'Justice'. Write down in each column the parts of the Magna Carta that belong in each column. The first one has been done for you.

What the Magna Carta said:

Religion	Taxes	Justice
John was not to interfere with the Church.		

Exercise 5.9

Read the two following sources and then answer the questions.

SOURCE A: based on the work of modern historian Nigel Saul.

> *In many ways John was the most resourceful of the sons of Henry II. He understood administration and did much to make it work better. He created the idea for a system of national taxation. And he brought into being the navy that thwarted King Philip's projected invasion. However, he failed in the art of managing men. Too often, he was slippery and untrustworthy.*

SOURCE B: based on the writing of Roger of Wendover, a monk in St. Albans who wrote a few years after John's death.

> *In 1209, a priest called Geoffrey said it was not safe for priests to work for the King any longer. John heard of this and Geoffrey was imprisoned in chains, clad in a cloak of lead and starved. Weakened and crushed, Geoffrey died an agonising death.*

1. According to Source A, why was John good?

2. According to Source B, why was John bad?

When asked if a source is reliable, a historian needs to think about a number of things: who produced the source, when and where was it produced, why did he or she produce it and what did he or she say or show in the source? This is called looking at the provenance of a source. Is Source A, written centuries after the death of King John more trustworthy than Source B, written by someone alive during the same time? Who is more reliable: a monk, alive at the time, who stayed in a monastery and listened to the gossip of travellers; or a modern historian, who has been able to look at both sides of an argument but is doing so hundreds of years after the time he is describing?

3. Look again at Sources A and B. Which source do you think is more reliable and why?

Chapter 6 Henry III and the Edwards

Henry III, 1216-1272

Imagine, at the age of nine, being told that you are the ruler of England and much of France. Nine-year-old Henry was told just that in 1216 when his father John died. But at the time, most of the French lands were lost and England itself was close to falling to the invading forces of Prince Louis, son of the King of France.

Young King Henry was lucky because some strong men stood by him, including the elderly William the Marshal, one of the most respected knights in all of Europe. The rebel barons who had been fighting his father did not wish to fight the boy King. Henry's men defeated the French forces at sea and Prince Louis decided to give up all hope of conquering England after defeat at the Battle of Lincoln in 1217. The civil war and the invasion were over.

Henry III; from the manuscript of Historia Anglorum by Matthew Paris, produced around 1255

Henry III was to be King for a very long time, from 1216 to 1272. Once grown up he was described as being of medium height and a strong build, with a drooping eyelid over one eye. He has often been remembered for being a foolish king who repeated the mistakes of his father. But how unsuccessful was Henry?

Henry's plans and successes

Henry III was ambitious, and not just about being the King of England. He had plans to retake his French lands and at the same time protect Gascony, which he still held. He worked to connect his family with other important rulers in Europe in order to restrict the power of King Louis of France and the Pope. However, he also believed strongly in the Church. He had Westminster Abbey rebuilt and agreed to go on crusade like his uncle, Richard I, before him.

However, things went wrong for Henry in dealing with his barons. Henry strongly believed that the king was the real power in the land. He had agreed to the Magna Carta, but he did not always agree with the barons about what it actually meant.

Henry used outsiders and foreigners to run his government, which angered many of his barons. At first, when the barons tried to make trouble, Henry was able to control them. For example, in 1233 William the Marshal's son Richard caused Henry problems but he died the following year. Many believed Henry had had the rebel baron killed.

By 1258, however, things were different. Henry had attempted to make his son King of Sicily but had failed. This had cost huge amounts of money and had angered the Pope, who threatened to excommunicate Henry. This and the anger about foreigners in control of the government led to a rebellion against Henry. Simon de Montfort was the key leader. Simon was a ruthless French baron who ruled Gascony for Henry. He was also the Earl of Leicester, a crusader, and married to Henry III's sister.

Under pressure from the rebels, that year Henry III and his son Edward were forced to swear an oath protecting England against foreigners and forcing Henry to rid himself of outsiders in government, including his own half-brothers from France. Known as the Provisions of Oxford, this oath meant that Henry was no longer in complete control as King, but had to do as the rebel barons wanted. These barons made their wishes known at what was called a **Parliament**. The Parliament (which took its name from the French *parler* = to talk) was a meeting of the most important men in the country in a great council. Soon some barons stopped supporting the changes as they found that, while they could now question and control the King's actions, men below them were now able to start questioning *them*. Still, Simon de Montfort carried on, convinced that God was on his side, even when the Pope gave

his support to Henry. In 1264, King Louis IX of France said that the Provisions of Oxford could not restrict the King. When Henry and Prince Edward managed to raise an army, de Montfort fought and defeated them at the Battle of Lewes, and the two royals became his prisoners.

De Montfort's position, however, was far from secure. Many in England now felt that he and his family were using their power simply to make themselves rich.

The Battle of Evesham, 4th August 1265; from a 19th century children's history book

Bringing together not only barons and churchmen, but also knights and townsmen in a Parliament to discuss issues usually reserved for the king was de Montfort's attempt to raise more support, but it was not enough. When Prince Edward managed to escape and join de Montfort's enemies, he forced him into battle at Evesham in 1265 and destroyed the rebel army. De Montfort and his closest associates were killed. King Henry himself only just escaped being killed by his own followers, as he had been dressed like de Montfort's men. Most of the de Montfort family were hunted down and their great stronghold of Kenilworth Castle was taken.

Although Henry continued to reign as King, he and the monarchs who succeeded him could no longer ignore the demands of the nobles and the other important leaders in England. The idea that a body of men, or Parliament, drawn from the nobility and common people, could advise the King and help him raise money, was to become the accepted state of affairs during the rule of Henry's son Edward I.

When Henry III died and was buried in the rebuilt Westminster Abbey in 1272 (near his hero Edward the Confessor), probably the most important thing he left, after the rebellions which had divided the country for so many years, was a land at peace.

Exercise 6.1
Match the phrases in each column to make correct sentences:

1. Henry III   (a) wanted his son to be King of Sicily.

2. Simon de Montfort   (b) won the Battle of Lewes.

3. The rebel barons   (c) was nine years old in 1216.

4. Prince Edward   (d) forced the King to accept the Provisions of Oxford in 1258.

5. Henry III   (e) won the Battle of Evesham.

Exercise 6.2
Write several sentences about each of the following:

1. Parliament

2. Prince Edward

3. Simon de Montfort

4. The Provisions of Oxford

5. The Battle of Evesham

Exercise 6.3

How successful was Henry III as a king? Next to each of the following points write several sentences explaining the extent to which they apply to Henry:

1. A good commander and warrior

2. Supporter and protector of the church

3. Just and fair

4. Left a son to rule after him

Exercise 6.4

Read the following extract, which is taken from the *Waverley Annals*, a contemporary chronicle. Then answer the questions.

> *When they arrived outside the town of Evesham, Prince Edward, the King's son, fell upon them with a large force of men. As soon as the King saw Edward, he withdrew himself, and fighting broke out on all sides. In the battle, that most worthy knight, Simon de Montfort, Earl of Leicester, his son Henry and Hugh Despenser, were among the many who were slain.*

1. What did Henry III do as the battle began?

2. Other than Simon de Montfort, who else was killed in the battle?

3. Sometimes we can guess the feelings of a contemporary writer by the way he describes people and events. What does the writer of the source say that gives us a clue to how he thought of Henry III and Simon de Montfort?

The three Edwards

The three King Edwards, Edward I, Edward II and Edward III, ruled England for a little over one hundred years. From the time of Edward I, the grandson of King John, to *his* grandson Edward III, life in the British Isles changed in many ways. But some things were to remain the same, particularly England's involvement in the affairs of France.

Edward I, 1272-1307

When Edward came to the throne in 1272, he already had a wealth of experience in helping his father Henry III deal with rebellion and in going on crusade to the Holy Land. The new King towered over his subjects not just as a great military leader, but because at over six feet tall he was deservedly called 'Longshanks'.

Edward I, known as Longshanks and the Hammer of the Scots, investing his son Edward (later Edward II) as Prince of Wales; from a 14th century manuscript

To the English he was to prove a king who had fewer problems in the country than his father or grandfather. No doubt this was because Edward understood the need to rule through the law and began to use Parliament to pass **statutes**, which became the most important laws of the land. Amongst the statutes or laws passed by Parliament under Edward I were those such as the Statute of Gloucester, which gave more power to the royal law courts rather than to the barons' courts.

However, Edward still made decisions without going to Parliament, passing, for example, the Statute of Mortmain which tried to restrict the amount of land given to the Church. And in 1290, Edward decided to confiscate the property of all the Jews living in England and to drive them from the country (see Chapter 7, page 108). This was probably in response to the growing need for money, but by the end of Edward's reign he was forced to concede that any attempt to raise taxes should be approved by Parliament.

We see a less ruthless side of Edward when his wife, Eleanor of Castile, died. He was so overcome with grief that he had memorial crosses built at every place the funeral party rested on its journey down to London. The sites of many of these are preserved to this day, the most famous being that at Charing Cross.

Edward I and the Welsh

If Edward did not always have his way in England, he proved to be a very effective soldier when dealing with other parts of the British Isles. He had a dream of uniting all the parts of Britain under himself as overlord.

An Eleanor Cross at Geddington, Northamptonshire

Parts of Wales had been under English control since the time of the Conquest in 1066. But during Henry III's rule, a Welsh prince called Llewelyn had managed to come close to creating a single Welsh princedom. This was not to be tolerated.

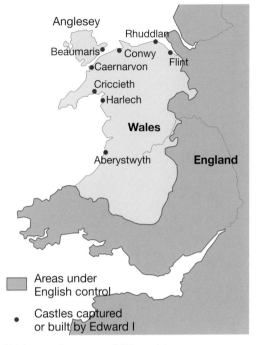

In 1274, Llewelyn refused to come to Edward and pay homage. As far as Edward was concerned Llewelyn owed him loyalty and service as King of England. When Llewelyn, who felt that Edward had wronged him, continued to refuse to pay homage, Edward lost his patience. In 1276-1277, three English armies invaded Wales. Many previous English attacks over the years had failed to defeat the Welsh amongst the mountains of Snowdonia, but

Wales at the time of Edward I

Edward had prepared well. He cut Llewelyn and his men off from the island of Anglesey, which had provided them with food, and forced them to come down from the northern Welsh mountains to surrender.

At first Edward simply forced Llewelyn to recognise him as his overlord. But Llewelyn soon found that he was being treated very much as an inferior and, in 1282, Llewelyn's brother David raised an army, took several castles and defeated the English forces. Although busy with France and Scotland, Edward took the time to raise a large army and once again seized Anglesey, before preparing to march into the Welsh mountains. Unluckily for the Welsh, Llewelyn was then killed almost by accident, and soon afterwards David was handed over to Edward. As Llewelyn's brother he was treated as a traitor and, after being found guilty in court, was hanged, drawn and quartered. This means he was hanged by the neck, but cut down before he died. He was then split open at the chest and his insides were removed. Finally, his body was cut into four sections to be displayed as a warning to others.

This time King Edward kept the Welsh lands for himself. To prevent further troubles he built a series of castles, mightier than any built before in the British Isles. The Welsh were forced to accept English law and their lands were divided into new counties under English officers. New towns were created, and they were settled by English people. The Welsh were not happy about this, but they were powerless to stop the English invasion.

Conwy Castle, built by Edward I in 1283

Edward I and Scotland

In Scotland, things were slightly different. Scotland was both an independent kingdom and a country closely linked to England. Many of its barons and knights held land in England and lived very much like the English. However, its close links with France helped keep Scotland separate from England and made it a potential threat to the English kings.

In 1279, the King of Scotland, Alexander III, paid homage to Edward. When Alexander died unexpectedly in 1286, leaving only his three-year-old granddaughter Margaret of Norway as next in line, Edward was asked to 'keep an eye' on the kingdom (see the family tree on p.??). Edward obliged and promptly arranged a marriage between Margaret and his own son, also named Edward. Trouble started, however, when Margaret died suddenly in 1290, leaving no clear heir to the throne of Scotland. Up to ninety different men stepped forward claiming to be the rightful king. The nobles in Scotland turned

Scotland at the time of Edward I and Edward II

to Edward to decide who was to be king. Of the three best candidates, John Baliol, Robert Bruce and John Hastings, Edward and his advisors decided on John Baliol, who was duly crowned and swore homage to Edward in 1292.

Edward had earlier agreed that Scotland was an independent kingdom, but he soon began to interfere in decisions made by King John. When the Scots made an alliance with France in 1295, Edward saw this as a betrayal by one of his vassals. At the same time that the Scots allied themselves with the French, Edward I was facing problems in France as the King of France had seized Gascony from his control. The Welsh at this time were also threatening to revolt (see page 82). The result was that Edward, determined to put Scotland once and for all under his control, invaded Scotland in 1296 and seized the town of Berwick. He defeated Baliol, publicly stripped him of his crown and imprisoned him in England. He also had the ancient Stone of Scone, the coronation stone of the kings of Scotland, taken back to England, where it was kept in Westminster Abbey for many centuries to come.

Many Scots were unhappy about Edward's control over Scotland. Several men rose up to fight the English, the most famous being William Wallace. Wallace held land in the lowlands of Scotland. The story goes that he argued with, and killed, an English official, thus becoming an outlaw. He then began to gather men to resist the English. Even though a major rebellion was stopped, men like Wallace kept the spirit of rebellion alive. When the English tried to stamp this out they were badly defeated at the Battle of Stirling Bridge in 1297, and the Scots began to raid into England. Edward was forced to put together a large army to deal with this threat and he defeated Wallace's army at the Battle of Falkirk in 1298. Still the Scots resisted. In 1304, having settled his dispute with King Philip in France, Edward took Stirling, the last great Scottish castle still holding out and, in 1305, William Wallace was betrayed by one of his own countrymen. He was taken to London, where he was executed and had his head placed on London Bridge.

Unfortunately for Edward the English were becoming tired of the fighting in Scotland faster than the Scots. In 1306, Robert Bruce, the grandson of the man who had claimed the Scottish throne in 1290, took up the Scottish cause. At one point Bruce was forced to hide in the Scottish wilderness. There he was supposed to have watched a spider rebuild its web every time it was destroyed, refusing to give in, and this gave Bruce new heart. The fighting was still going on when Edward, 67 years old, died in northern England in 1307, while preparing to lead his army once more into Scotland.

Exercise 6.5

Copy the paragraph below, filling in the blanks.

Edward I was crowned in _____. Unlike his father _____ he did not have many problems and was happy to use parliament to pass _____. He was very harsh to the _____, whom he drove out of the country. Edward was forced by his nobles to agree that _____ had to agree to any attempts to raise _____.

Exercise 6.6

1. Study the map and match the numbers 1-5 with the places (a)-(e):

    1. Anglesey
    2. Berwick
    3. Falkirk
    4. Snowdonia
    5. Stirling Castle

2. Now write a sentence or two about how each of the five places above played a part in Edward's invasions of Wales and Scotland.

Exercise 6.7

1. Write a paragraph explaining how and why Edward took Wales.

2. Write a paragraph explaining how and why Edward tried to take Scotland.

3. Write a paragraph about Parliament, explaining how Edward I used Parliament when ruling the country.

Exercise 6.8

Read the sources below and answer the questions which follow:

SOURCE A: From the chronicle *Historia Anglicana*, written by Bartholomew Cotton, a monk at the time.

> At this time, [1290] an edict went out from the King throughout England that, after 1st November, no Jews should remain in the land upon pain of death and that, if any Jew were to be found there subsequently, he should be beheaded.

SOURCE B: From William Rishanger, a monk of St. Albans Abbey who was a contemporary of Edward I, concerning Edward's reaction to the death of his wife, Queen Eleanor.

For the rest of his days he mourned for her, and offered unceasing prayers on her behalf... He gave generous grants of alms and celebrations of Mass for her in various places around the kingdom.

The King gave orders that, in every place where her funeral carriage had rested, a cross of the finest workmanship should be erected in her memory, so that passers-by might pray for her soul.

SOURCE C: From the chronicle of Peter Langtoft, a monk from Bridlington, who wrote in French verse.

King Edward was the flower of Christendom.
He was so handsome and great, so powerful in arms,
That of him may one speak as long as the world lasts.
For he had no equal as a knight in armour
For vigour and valour, neither present nor future.

1. Look at Source A. What would happen to any Jew still in the country after 1st November?

2. Look at Source B. What different things did King Edward I do in memory of his wife?

3. Look at Source C. Write down at least three words that the author used to describe Edward I.

4. With which of the other sources does Source C *disagree* the most? Make sure you carefully compare each of the sources to Source C, using quotations where possible.

Edward II, 1307-1327

Edward II was a rather different sort of king from his warlike father. Tall like his father, he did not, however, have his intelligence, and proved to be very dependent upon favourites. The first of these was Piers Gaveston, a knight from Gascony. Many of the barons, led by Thomas, Earl of Lancaster, tried to develop their power and influence in governing England and forced the King to accept their advice as to who held important jobs. They also forced Edward to send Gaveston into exile. When Edward tried to break the barons' power by bringing him back, Gaveston was executed by Lancaster's men.

While Edward was busy with these problems in England, Robert Bruce took the opportunity to continue to drive the English out of Scotland, and also to make raids deep into northern England. In 1314, the Scots threatened one of the final English strongholds, Stirling Castle, forcing the barons and Edward to put aside their quarrel and to raise an army. With perhaps as many as 20 000 men, Edward's army met Bruce's much smaller army at Bannockburn, near Stirling Castle.

Edward II; from the manuscript of Piers Langtoft's History of England, produced around 1300

The Battle of Bannockburn, 1314

At the Battle of Bannockburn, Edward II's large army was made up of mounted knights and a large number of foot soldiers, including Welsh archers. The Scots had between 6000 and 10 000 men, with only a small body of mounted knights. They depended

Robert Bruce and Sir Henry de Bohun on the eve of the Battle of Bannockburn; from a 19th century children's history book

upon blocks of foot soldiers called **schiltrons**, armed with long spears. Bruce chose his battlefield well, as Edward's army had to cross a stream, called Bannock Burn, before reaching his men. The battlefield was also hemmed in by marshy ground, making it impossible for the mounted English knights to ride around the Scottish line.

On 23rd June, the day before the main battle began, Robert Bruce was caught riding in front of his army by an English knight, Sir Henry de Bohun, who tried to ride him down with his lance.

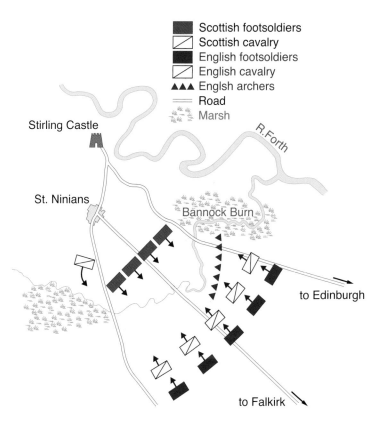

Scottish footsoldiers
Scottish cavalry
English footsoldiers
English cavalry
▲▲▲ **English archers**
══ **Road**
Marsh

Stirling Castle

St. Ninians

R. Forth

Bannock Burn

to Edinburgh

to Falkirk

The Battle of Bannockburn, 24th June 1314

Bruce, armed with a battle-axe, coolly moved aside as de Bohun thundered down upon him, and as he rode past, slammed his axe down and split the knight's head open.

The next day many of the English nobles and knights proved impatient to fight the Scots and pushed forward, leaving the archers to the rear where they could not fire effectively. The mounted English quickly found that they could not break the Scottish schiltrons, and yet the English further back could not advance to fight. When the English and Welsh archers managed to find a place to the side of the line to begin firing, the Scottish mounted troops swiftly charged and swept them away.

The battle continued for some time as the English tried to break the Scottish line and the Scots stubbornly resisted. Then the English spotted a large number of people moving to join the Scottish defence (these were in fact mostly camp followers, the young, the sick and the women). Believing these to be reinforcements, many of Edward's army panicked and tried to flee, only to be cut down by the chasing Scots or drowned in the burn and marshes. Edward himself only narrowly escaped.

The return of favourites: the Despensers

The defeat at Bannockburn meant that Edward was now at the mercy of his barons. Lancaster more or less ran the government for a while, but the King wanted to restore royal power and showed this by again finding favourites, this time in Hugh Despenser and his son, also called Hugh. Their greed in taking lands for themselves helped lead to a rebellion in 1321, when Edward was forced to send the Despensers into exile. But the King struck back swiftly in late 1321, raising an army and defeating Lancaster's forces in 1322. Thomas of Lancaster was captured and beheaded as a traitor.

At this point, all the efforts of the barons to try to control the power of English kings seemed to have failed. In 1322 the Statute of York was passed, stating that the king's subjects could never force reforms that were against royal power. Parliament remained, but its powers were limited.

However, things soon changed again for Edward. His wife, Queen Isabella, sometimes called the She-Wolf of France, was the daughter of Philip IV, King of France. She had been engaged to Edward II when she was just twelve years old. Isabella produced four children, but much of her married life she spent being jealous of Edward's favourites such as Gaveston and the Despensers. When she was asked to help settle Edward's problems in Gascony by talking to the French King, her brother, she seized her chance to join with a rebel English lord, Roger Mortimer, against her husband.

When she sailed from France to England with a small force, not a finger was raised to support Edward. His failures as a warrior king, his use of favourites, the struggle with the barons – all of these things had turned the entire country against him. The Despensers were hunted down and executed, the Bishop of Exeter, a supporter of Edward's, was dragged off his horse in London and beheaded, and Edward himself was captured and forced, fearful and weeping, to give up his throne in favour of his fourteen-year-old son, the future Edward III. However, as long as he remained alive, Edward II continued to be a threat to Isabella and Mortimer, so it is not surprising that within a year he was dead. The death of Edward II at Berkeley Castle in 1327 was probably ordered by the Queen and Mortimer. How he died is not totally clear, but one story is that he was murdered with a red hot wire or poker.

Exercise 6.9

Write a sentence or two about each of the following:

1. Piers Gaveston

2. Thomas, Earl of Lancaster

3. Robert Bruce (the younger)

4. The Statute of York

5. The Despensers

Exercise 6.10

Why did Edward II fail as a king?

1. Make a list of reasons for Edward's failure.

2. Put the reasons in order, the first being the most important. Why did you choose this reason?

Edward III, 1327-1377

In many ways, Edward III was like his grandfather. He has become known as one of England's great warrior kings, along with Richard I and Edward I. But when he became king at fifteen, he was very much under the control of his mother Queen Isabella and her lover Roger Mortimer. Between them, Isabella and Roger ruled on his behalf, and the money that Edward II had collected was soon spent, leaving the young King with major financial trouble. At seventeen, however, Edward, with a group of young noble friends, burst into the Queen's bedroom and arrested Mortimer. Mortimer was found guilty of treason and executed. Queen Isabella was sent to live the rest of her days in a castle in Norfolk. She was buried in London in 1358 in the habit of a nun.

Edward III; from a 15th century manuscript

At first, Edward made some of the same mistakes as his father, by relying on a small group of friends to the anger of most of the barons. But, over the years, Edward learned that the best way to control England was to find a task that all Englishmen could join in, with him as their leader. That task was to be the pursuit of the throne of France.

The start of the Hundred Years' War

There were a number of reasons for the outbreak of war against the King of France:

- There had been more fighting against the Scots, who were receiving aid from the French.

- The English kings' control of Gascony was resented by the kings of France.

- The death, without children, of the last French king, Charles IV, meant that Edward III had a claim to the French throne through his mother Isabella, Charles's sister. However, the crown was given to Philip VI of Valois.

- Against this background, Edward was facing threats towards his French lands.

When the war broke out in 1337, Edward's first efforts gained very little, and cost him a great deal of money. In fact, the French successfully raided the south coast of England in 1338 and 1339 and threatened an invasion. Edward had spent all his money, and had to leave his wife and children in Antwerp as hostages until he could pay back his loans.

Having talked Parliament into raising more money, Edward set sail with a fleet to attack the larger French fleet off the town of Sluys. On 24th June 1340, the English ships attacked. The French had anchored their ships in three lines, and were unable to move to react to the English. Although he was slightly wounded in the battle, Edward led his forces to a great victory, with nearly 18 000 Frenchmen killed in the battle. The men in the court of Philip VI were frightened to tell their master about the defeat at Sluys. Finally the court jester asked the King a riddle: 'Why are the English more cowardly than the French?' When the King was unable to reply, the jester uttered the fateful words: 'Because the English do not jump into the sea with their armour on.' Philip then understood that he had lost his fleet.

On land, however, Edward was not doing well, losing more of Gascony. Money was again becoming short. But, as things gradually improved for Edward in the south of France, he decided to invade France from the north.

The Crécy campaign, 1346

The Crécy campaign began when Edward gathered an army of about 15 000 men and, in July 1346, landed his force in Normandy. The King marched and sailed along the coast, plundering and destroying. He then marched inland, taking the town of Caen and sacking it, killing 3000 of its citizens. The English were certainly terrifying the French and gathering riches, but this was not helping Edward's claim as King.

As Edward's army marched on east and north, it came to the River Seine. King Philip VI of France, who had gathered a large army at Rouen, was trying to cut off the English by destroying all the bridges. Marching on the south bank of the river, plundering and destroying as they went, the English were forced ever closer to Paris in search of a crossing. There was panic in Paris as the English came within 20 miles, but Edward only wanted to cross the Seine. At Poissy, enough of the bridge survived for the English to rebuild it, and they crossed on 15th August.

King Edward now led his force north. Philip followed, marching hard and reaching the River Somme first. Again the French attempted to destroy or guard all the crossing places to force the smaller English

The Battle of Sluys, 24th June 1340; from a 15th century manuscript of Jean Froissart's Chronicle

army into battle. The English had to move further west towards the coast, as they were unable to cross the river and their food and supplies were fast running out. Philip had moved most of his army onto the south side of the Somme and was marching to catch Edward. However, the English learned of a tidal ford at Blanchetaque and forced their way through the French guards.

Edward knew that the French were now too close, and that it was futile to keep running. The time had come to choose a battlefield. Just beyond the village of Crécy, on 26th August, he placed his army on a ridge facing south-east, using a windmill as his command post. It is estimated that Edward had around 12 000 men.

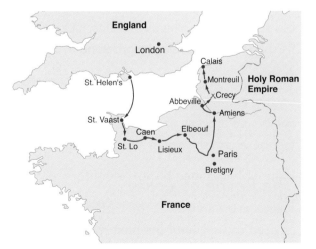

The Crécy campaign, 1346

The armies

The English army had a small number of knights and mounted men at arms, heavily armoured in a mixture of **mail** and **plate armour**. Plate armour was made of thin but solid steel and, although heavier, gave much better protection to its wearer than ring mail. The English depended upon archers, equipped with the **longbow**. The longbow was 1.8 metres (6 feet) in length and made of wood such as yew. Although the crossbow could fire further, the longbow could launch ten or more arrows a minute, making it much quicker than the crossbow. Used in large enough numbers and with the right kind of arrowheads, the longbow arrows could penetrate mail and plate armour, causing major problems to attacking armoured men.

A knight of the 14th century

An English bowman of the 14th century

The English had learned, while fighting against the Welsh and Scots, that mounted charges by knights were not as effective as dismounted knights fighting alongside large groups of archers. They waited for the French in two large groups in front of the windmill under the commands of the Earl of Northampton and Edward's sixteen-year-old son, Edward Prince of Wales, nicknamed 'The Black Prince'. King Edward himself held another smaller group behind in reserve.

The French army had perhaps 30 000 to 40 000 men, consisting largely of mounted knights and men-at-arms. These men saw warfare as a chance to display their fighting ability and bravery, and were not easy to control. There was also a large force of hired Genoese crossbowmen, but the French knights thought little of their ability.

The Battle of Crécy

Philip's army arrived at the battlefield late on 26th August 1346 and the King was advised to wait until the next morning, as many of his men were still some distance away. But the nobles in the front of the army felt it was shameful to retreat and more French knights were arriving all the time and pushing forward. Philip felt he had no choice but to attack and sent the crossbowmen forward. There was a rain shower as they advanced, wetting their bowstrings (the English kept theirs dry) and to make matters worse, the Genoese found they were firing into the setting sun. The English archers, on higher ground and in greater numbers, showered arrows upon the Genoese, who began to retreat, only to be trampled by the French cavalry who were moving up into position behind them, ready to charge. Again the English longbowmen sent flights of arrows

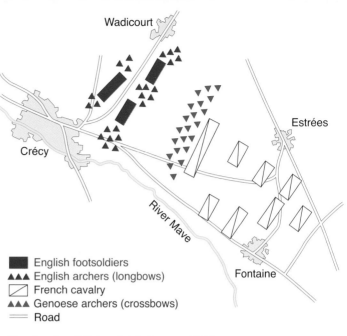

English footsoldiers
▲▲▲ English archers (longbows)
◢ French cavalry
▲▲▲ Genoese archers (crossbows)
═══ Road

The Battle of Crécy, 26th August 1346

into the attackers, particularly striking the less protected horses. Knights and nobles spilled onto the ground to be trampled by their own side. As soon as the first charge was broken, another came, and then another. The English archers kept up their bloody work, but some brave French knights managed to reach the English lines. At one point word reached King Edward that his son needed help. According to one writer of the time Edward refused, saying that he wanted the Prince of Wales to 'earn his spurs'. (Another writer reported that the King did send twenty knights, who found the Black Prince and his comrades leaning on their weapons and surrounded by French bodies.)

In all, the French charged fifteen or more times, until it was too dark to see. King Philip, who had had a horse killed under him and had been wounded, was led from the battlefield. Another king, blind John of Luxembourg, King of Bohemia, was an ally of the French and insisted that his followers lead him into the battle. His body was found the next day, still tied to his men. The Prince of Wales was so moved by this that he took for himself John's symbol of three feathers, and to this day the Prince of Wales has three feathers as part of his crest.

The end of the campaign

The English victory at Crécy was overwhelming. The French lost 10 000 men, including Philip VI's younger brother and 1500 lords and knights. English losses were several hundred dead or wounded. But the campaign was not over and Edward was still not King of France.

King Edward decided that he needed to control a French port. He marched on Calais as he believed it would fall quickly. But Calais was commanded by a strong leader, Jean de Vienne, had stout walls and was surrounded by marshy land. For long months the town held out, while the one attempt made by the English to fight their way in failed. The English army grew to 30 000 men besieging Calais and, by the summer of 1347, the defenders were starving. When de Vienne sent several hundred women, children, elderly and sick people out from the town, Edward refused to let them pass and they were left to die just outside the town walls. Philip VI finally appeared on the cliffs above the town in July 1347, but was badly outnumbered by the English. Unable to do anything to help, his army marched away.

Edward III and the six burghers of Calais; from a 15th century manuscript

With no help, Calais was forced to surrender. Jean de Vienne and Edward's commanders managed to convince the King not to kill all the soldiers and citizens of Calais, but Edward did demand that six of the most important townsmen ('burghers') were to bring him the keys of the city, wearing only white shirts and with rope halters around their necks. When they arrived Edward ordered their heads to be cut off, but Queen Philippa pleaded for their lives and the men were spared. However, they and all the other inhabitants of Calais lost all their property and were forced to leave the town, which was resettled by the English. With a truce in September Edward returned to England a hero.

Throughout the rest of Edward III's long rule, the Hundred Years' War continued on and off. When the Black Death struck Europe in 1348, it caused both sides to pause for several years.

Edward's rule became more and more dependent upon doing well in fighting the French, as this kept the nobles happy, giving them a chance to achieve great riches in plunder and in capturing and ransoming important French knights and lords. The greatest catch of all came with the Battle of Poitiers on 19th September 1356, when the Black Prince fought a much larger French army under the new French King John II, and captured John himself.

Edward III and Parliament

In spite of these victories, Edward was no closer to becoming King of France, and not everybody was happy. Even though Parliament provided money for the King, there were protests about the heavy taxation. Edward had learned that he needed to appear to give something to his Parliaments to earn their support. He was the first monarch to address Parliament in English and he allowed Parliament more control over taxation.

By 1376, Edward was an old and feeble man. The war in France was going badly, and all that the English had of France

The French campaigns of the Black Prince

was a narrow strip of Gascony and the town of Calais. Queen Philippa had died some time before, and Edward had fallen under the influence of Alice Perrers who, along with several advisors, was accused of taking advantage of the old King. Because of the need for taxes, Parliament was called and for once it was the Commons, not the Lords, who took the lead. Parliament demanded reforms, including the removal of the bad advisors, before any money would be raised. John of Gaunt, one of Edward III's sons, argued strongly against the reforms, but they were popular with the people and the process came to be known as the Good Parliament. Nonetheless, John of Gaunt used his influence to reverse many of the reforms within a year. By 1377 the advisors had returned and the Commons' leader was imprisoned.

The death of Edward III

The King's death in 1377 left England in some difficulties. His eldest son, the Black Prince, had died shortly before of disease caught while leading troops in France. Next in line to the throne was the Black Prince's son, Richard, a nine-year-old boy (see the family tree on page 169). Crowned King Richard II, he inherited the glories of his grandfather's successes, but also the problems caused by the Black Death, heavy taxes and the growing French successes in the war.

Exercise 6.11

Write out the following paragraphs, filling in the blanks:

Edward III became King after his mother _____ _____ and her lover _____ _____ seized power from _____. After taking control, Edward had to deal with problems on his northern border with _____. He was also having problems with the King of France over control of _____. This helped lead to the outbreak of the _____ _____ War. Edward III had some successes against the French king, including the naval battle at _____ and at the Battle of _____. The war was halted when the _____ _____ struck both France and England.

At the end of his reign, however, the _____ _____ in 1376 showed that not every Englishman was happy. Because the _____ _____ had also died, Edward III's death meant that nine-year-old _____ was to be the next king.

Exercise 6.12

Write a sentence or two about each of the following:

1.   Philip VI of France

2.   The Battle of Sluys

3.   The Seige of Calais

4.   The Battle of Poitiers

5.   The Good Parliament

Exercise 6.13

Read the following sources, then answer the questions:

SOURCE A: Written by Geoffrey le Baker, a monk who had talked to Thomas de la Moore, a knight who fought for Edward III at Crécy.

> *When they saw that their crossbowmen were not harming the English at all, the French men-at-arms rode down the crossbowmen. They crushed them beneath the feet of their horses, and charged headlong forward...*

SOURCE B: Written by Jean Froissart, a French priest born in 1337 who travelled widely to research his writings. He produced his work for Edward's wife Philippa of Hainault, and claimed to have spoken to people who were actually at the battle.

[The Genoese] advanced with their crossbows presented, and began to shoot. The English archers then advanced one step forward, and shot their arrows with such force and quickness that it seemed as if it snowed. When the Genoese felt these arrows which pierced through their armour, some of them cut the strings of their crossbows, others flung them to the ground, and all turned about and retreated quite discomfited.

The French had a large body of men-at-arms on horseback to support the Genoese, and the King, seeing them thus fall back, cried out, "Kill me those scoundrels, for they stop up our road without any reason." The English continued shooting and, some of their arrows falling among the horsemen, drove them upon the Genoese so that they were in such confusion, they could never rally again.

SOURCE C is a picture of the Battle of Crécy from a 15th century chronicle.

1. Look at Source A. What happened to the crossbowmen?

2. Look at Source B. How did the Genoese react when the English archers fired upon them?

3. Look at Source C. What does it show happening? Does this agree or disagree with what each of the other sources say? How does it support what the other sources say about the crossbowmen?

4. Look at all the sources. Remember to look at who produced each source and when, and think about how much each author would know. Was he an eyewitness? Are there clues that any of the authors were one-sided concerning the battle?

The Battle of Crécy; from a 15th century manuscript

Now write a paragraph comparing all three sources and judging which source would be the most useful to a historian wanting to know what happened to the Genoese crossbowmen. Remember that by the term 'useful' we mean both the extent to which we can trust the source *and* the kind of information it gives the reader. While a source may not always give a truthful or balanced account, it might very well tell the reader a lot about the viewpoint of the person or people who produced it.

Chapter 7 Life in the Middle Ages

Before we move on to find out what happened after the death of Edward III, we are now going to step back and look at life in the Middle Ages. What was it like to be alive at that time? We will start with the building that perhaps more than anything else sums up this period of history: the castle.

Castles

Castles have always been seen as part of the landscape of the Middle Ages. Most people think of a castle as a great stone building, the home of a king, with banners flying as mounted knights thunder across the wooden drawbridge to the sound of trumpets. But is this really what castles were like? And why were they actually built?

Early castles

As you learned in Chapter 2, the first castles were not built of stone at all. In 1066, the Norman invaders needed quick and ready bases from which to control a hostile England, and so constructed the motte and bailey castles, made of earthworks and wood. These provided a home for groups of mounted men who could ride out and keep control of the local Saxon population. They were also the high security residences of Norman barons and were carefully positioned to control key places such as river crossings or towns. Their great weaknesses, however, were rot and fire and they did not last much more than twenty years.

The tower keep at Rochester Castle

The shell keep at Tamworth Castle

When motte and bailey castles fell into disrepair, their owners were usually prepared to build more permanent structures. For example, wooden palisades or walls could be replaced by stone **curtain walls**; and the motte could have a **shell keep** placed on top, or be replaced with a **tower keep**.

How to attack and defend castles

During medieval times, most wars were not fought with lots of big battles, but consisted instead of a succession of **sieges** to capture castles and fortified towns. New ways of attacking castles and town walls were developed, and new defences were invented to counter these attacks.

As you might expect, the simplest way to take a castle was to go through the doorway or gate. Consequently, defenders developed a whole series of ways to make doing this as difficult as possible.

Here are some of the things that they built; can you work out how they made defending the entrance easier?

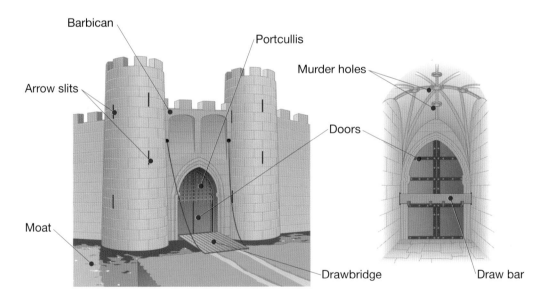

An artist's impression of the entrance to a 14th century castle

There might be a deep ditch, or **moat** filled with water, which would have a **drawbridge** over it. The castle defenders would simply raise the drawbridge when attacked. And if the defenders were taken by surprise, they could use a **portcullis** that would drop down quickly and seal off the doorway. If they had more time, heavy wooden doors would be closed and locked with a **drawbar**. But, as the entrance was still the weakest part of a castle, more defences could be added. Towers could be built on either side of the gateway so that defenders could fire down on anyone trying to reach the doorway. **Murder holes** could be set in the ceiling of the gateway so that objects and boiling liquids could be poured down on attackers, and attempts to set the door on fire could be resisted. In some castles, the entrance was built like a tunnel, with arrow slits on the side, murder holes above and with several portcullises and heavy doors. A finishing touch might be to build a **barbican**, an outer gatehouse that would have to be broken into before the attackers even reached the main entrance.

If a castle could not be taken by coming through the entrance, the attackers might try to climb over the walls, using ladders. Stone curtain walls were made which were much higher than wooden walls and had **battlements** on top. A ditch or moat in front of the wall also made it hard to attack.

Because of all these defences, attackers developed other ways of attacking the walls. One method was to rush to the bottom of the wall and begin to dig away at it. To counter this, the castle builders began to make the bottom of the walls thicker, making it harder for them to be attacked. The defenders would lean over the battlements and fire downwards onto the attackers. However, this exposed the defenders and made them into targets for attacking bowmen. The designers then began to build towers along the walls that stuck out, allowing archers to fire downwards and sideways along the bottom of the wall, while still remaining under cover. Yet another defensive trick was to build wooden scaffolding, called a **hoarding**, out from the top of the wall, which allowed defenders to fire down on anyone directly underneath them.

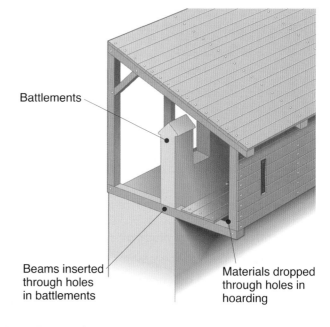

Battlements

When attackers tried to drag siege towers, or **belfries**, up to the wall so that they could jump over the battlements and attack the defenders, the defenders sometimes tried to build up their walls higher while under attack. Much more successful, however, was to make it impossible to use belfries by digging ditches or a moat around the castle, or building it on a hill.

Beams inserted through holes in battlements

Materials dropped through holes in hoarding

Hoardings: defences to protect the castle walls

Another trick used by attackers was to dig under the walls or a tower of a castle. The idea was that, when the tunnel collapsed, the wall or tower above would fall down, leaving a gap, or **breach**, that the attackers could use to rush in. One method that castle builders developed to counter this was to make the towers round, as square-shaped towers would easily collapse but round ones did not. Also, the round shape of the tower allowed defenders to see and fire at attackers much more easily.

Attacking a castle; a modern artist's impression

Another way to make a breach was to knock a hole in a wall with a **battering ram**. This weapon was basically a large log with an iron head that was pounded against the wall. Given enough time, it could punch through, but to reach the wall the attackers might have to fill in a ditch or moat and would find it hard to reach walls built at the top of a slope. It was much easier to break down stone walls by smashing through them from a distance. To do this the attackers could use a number of machines. Some, like the stone-throwing **mangonel**, were based on devices used by the ancient Greeks and Romans. The new invention of the medieval period was the **trebuchet**, which

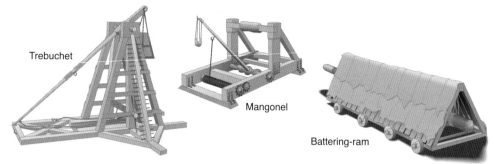

Trebuchet

Mangonel

Battering-ram

Ways to attack the castle walls

could hurl large stones or flaming materials at or over a wall. The problem with all these machines was that they had to be constructed by the attackers at the siege, because it was far too difficult to move such heavy devices for long distances.

Because of the difficulties of breaching the defences of a well-fortified town or castle, most attackers relied on **besieging** to gain entry. This involved surrounding it so that no-one could get in or out, and trying to starve out the defenders. If a castle or town was well prepared with food and other supplies, this might take months and the attackers could run out of food themselves or suffer from disease. There was also a chance that another army might arrive to rescue the defenders.

Because castles could be so difficult to take, kings tried to control who built them. A castle held by a rebel baron could be a major headache and take a long time and a lot of money to capture. Castles could also help a king and his barons control a troublesome area, like the borders with Wales and Scotland. When Edward I conquered north Wales, he had a series of castles made that were the strongest ever

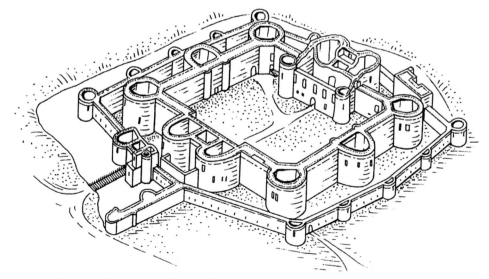

Concentric defences at Beaumaris Castle. How hard would it have been to enter this castle?

built in Britain. These were **concentric** castles, called this because they had defences within defences. By this time, the walls and towers of castles were so strongly built that keeps were no longer needed, because each tower became a keep in its own right.

Life in castles

Although castles were built for defence, they were really just very well-guarded homes. A castle might never be attacked, but would provide a living place for many people. Inside the strong walls were all the things needed for ordinary life. There would be a well, perhaps in the keep itself, like in the Tower of London and Rochester Castle. There would be a chapel for prayers. The lord of the castle and his family needed a place to live and this was provided by a hall, a large room that would serve as a meeting area, dining room, and even bedroom. The castle's servants and soldiers

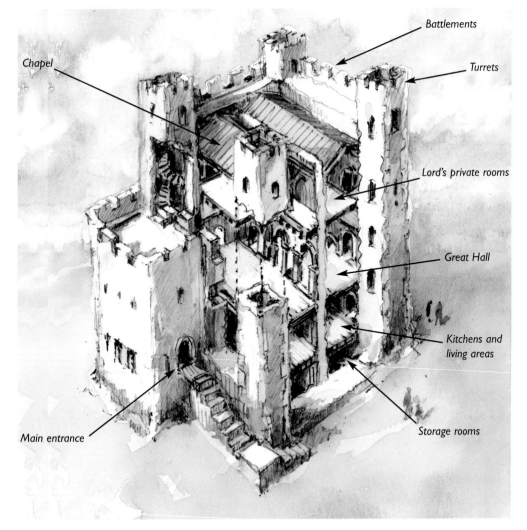

Battlements

Chapel

Turrets

Lord's private rooms

Great Hall

Kitchens and living areas

Storage rooms

Main entrance

Inside a tower keep

all slept in the hall. Castle halls were some of the first places to have fireplaces with chimneys so that more rooms, or even another hall, could be built above them. The lord and his family often had a smaller, private room, called a **solar**, where they could sleep. Many castles had more than one hall so that the man watching over the castle for his lord, the **castellan**, would have a place for his family to live, as well as halls for his lord and other important visitors. The large towers along the walls of some castles also provided places for people to live. Just like some modern high-rise buildings with penthouses, the higher you lived in a keep or tower, the more important you were. This was because higher up there was no need to have slit windows, so that important people could enjoy much more light with bigger openings. Some of these windows might even have had glass, but most windows were open to the air and were closed with wooden shutters.

A kitchen with fireplaces and ovens for cooking would be near the main hall, but not too close because of the threat of fire. The supplies needed for both ordinary life and for sieges would be kept in the cellars of the keep and towers of a castle. Normally, however, the number of people living in a castle, including soldiers, would be very small, perhaps only twenty in a place like Rochester Castle, a royal castle guarding the important road from London to Dover. Mighty Dover Castle, guarding the coast, would have had more but, unless an attack was coming, the numbers would still be small. The servants would be responsible for cooking, cleaning and general household chores. Men were usually part of the garrison defending the castle, though in times of peace they also took on some of the servants' duties.

The end of castles

Many people think that the end of castles came with the coming of gunpowder and cannons. This undoubtedly had an effect but, during the English Civil Wars, more than a hundred years after the end of the Middle Ages, many castles proved hard to take, even when the attackers did have cannons. But the fact is that, by the late medieval period, nobles and monarchs who lived in castles no longer felt they needed so much protection. Castles were simply not very comfortable places to live. Instead of building more defences, nobles began creating homes to live in, eventually leading to the great country houses which began to appear across the country, particularly from the reign of Elizabeth I. Many castles were left to rot. Some lasted until the 1640s and were used in the Civil Wars, but were then slighted (deliberately damaged or destroyed) to make sure they could not be used as forts again. Only a few, such as the Tower of London, Windsor Castle and Warwick Castle, continued to be lived in until modern times.

Exercise 7.1

Write a sentence or two about each of the following:

1.   Motte

2.   Curtain walls

3.   Portcullis

4.   Murder holes

5.   Barbican

Exercise 7.2

What were the advantages and disadvantages of living in a castle? Make a chart listing both.

Exercise 7.3

Read the source below and then answer the questions.

An account of the siege of Rochester that occurred in 1216, written by Roger of Wendover, a monk of St. Albans, between 1230-1236. The castle was being held by rebel barons who were trying to place Prince Louis of France on the throne (see pages 74/75).

> The King did not allow the besieged any rest day or night. For, among the stones hurled from the engines, and the missiles of the crossbows and archers, frequent attacks were made by knights and their followers, so that when some were tired, other fresh ones succeeded them in the assault; and with these changes the besieged had no rest.

> The besieged, too, tried to delay their own destruction. They feared greatly the cruelty of the King... The siege was lengthened many days owing to the great bravery and boldness of the besieged, who hurled stone for stone, weapon for weapon, from the walls on the enemy.

> At last, after great numbers of royal troops had been slain, the King, seeing his engines had little effect, employed miners, who soon threw down a great part of the walls. The besieged ran out of food, and were forced to eat their horses. The soldiers of the King now rushed to the breaches in the walls, and by constant fierce assaults they forced the besieged to abandon the castle [walls], though not without great loss on their own side. The besieged then entered the keep.

The King then applied his miners to the keep and, having after much difficulty broken through the walls, an opening was made for the attackers. While the King's miners were thus employed, they were often forced to retreat from the destruction caused in their ranks by the besieged.

At length, not a morsel of provisions remaining amongst them, the besieged, thinking it would be a disgrace to die of hunger when they could not be conquered in battle, surrendered.

1. Make a list of the different ways that the King attacked Rochester Castle.

2. Which other ways of attacking a castle were not used against Rochester Castle?

3. Explain, using quotations from the source, what the most successful method was of taking Rochester Castle.

4. What did the author of the source feel about the two sides? Support your answer by using quotations from the source.

The medieval underdogs: Jews and women

Medieval Britain was a place where, at least at first glance, men held power and Christianity was accepted by all. How true was this really?

The Jews

The first known presence of a Jewish community in medieval Britain was shortly after the Norman Conquest, centred in London. Although the Roman Catholic Church was hostile to these Jewish families, the kings gave them protection. The kings and other important men, including churchmen, needed to be able to borrow money. But the Church believed that money lending for profit, called **usury**, was wrong. Some Christians such as the Italian Medici family in the late Middle Ages did lend money, but wealthy Jewish traders were the main lenders during the eleventh to thirteenth centuries. By the time of Henry II there were Jewish communities scattered throughout the towns of the kingdom and

The Jews' Passover; a painting by a 15th century Dutch artist

they were generally tolerated as providers of a useful service. Kings like Henry II found the Jews doubly useful as heavy taxes could be raised from them without an outcry from the barons.

After Henry II the Jewish communities came under increasing pressure. When some wealthy Jews attempted to bring presents to Richard I on his coronation the surrounding crowd turned on and slaughtered them, then went on to burn and loot Jewish properties in London. Whilst King Richard executed the ringleaders of this outrage, further attacks occurred in several towns in East Anglia. During this time of the crusades many living in Britain saw the Jews as well as Muslims as the enemy. Some churchmen encouraged this belief with false stories of Christian children being kidnapped and murdered in Jewish rituals. These false stories became a tradition known as **blood libel**, and writers produced anti-Jewish literature and cartoons. This type of material, that encourages people to think a certain way, is called **propaganda**. In some cases those who owed money to Jewish moneylenders may have played a role in encouraging attacks. In 1190 the Jewish community in York was attacked and the surviving families sought shelter in the castle. There, surrounded by the mob, most of the Jews decided to take their lives rather than convert to Christianity. Nearly a hundred and fifty men, women and children died and the few who believed the mob's promise of mercy if they converted were murdered on the spot.

These anti-Jewish attacks, or **pogroms**, happened again in London and elsewhere in 1264. Meanwhile, more and more restrictions were placed upon the Jewish communities, forcing them to wear two strips of yellow cloth to mark them out, not allowing them to eat with Christians and even not allowing them out of their houses during Easter when anti-Jewish feelings were at their height. In 1275, in the first parliament of the new King Edward III, a new restriction was placed on the Jews as recorded by the monkish chronicler Thomas Wykes:

> After due consideration, a new law was imposed upon Jews living in England, for they were enemies of the Cross and they burdened Catholic Christians with intolerable heavy rates of interest. Henceforth, Jews were not to loan any money at interest, but should provide their means of life by the toil of their own hands and by lawful business.

Stopped from creating more wealth, yet faced with crippling taxes, the Jewish communities in Britain were on the verge of disaster. Many Jews were accused of clipping, or taking slices of silver from coins; three hundred were hanged in 1279. As we learned in Chapter 6 (page 82), the final blow came in 1290, as described in Bartholomew Cotton's *Historia Anglicana*, written at the time:

At this time an edict went out from the king throughout England that, after
1st November, no Jews should remain in the land upon pain of death and that, if any
Jew were to be found there afterwards, he should be beheaded.

No longer useful, the Jews were thrown out of Britain, not to return in any numbers for nearly four centuries.

Exercise 7.4

Write a sentence or two about each of the following:

1. Usury

2. Pogroms

3. Propaganda

4. Blood libel

5. The Medici family

Exercise 7.5

Read the following source and answer the questions:

SOURCE A: From *The Canterbury Tales* by Geoffrey Chaucer.

> *In Asia was a great Christian city*
> *With a Jewish quarter maintained*
> *By the great lord who governed them*
> *By foul usury and shameful profits.*
> *Hateful to Christ, and hated by Christians,*
> *Though people passed through their street*
> *As either end was free and open…*
> *All the Jews conspired*
> *To hunt to death an innocent young boy,*
> *And so they hired a murderer*
> *Who hid himself in an alleyway.*
> *This cursed Jew seized and held him*
> *Cut his throat, and threw him in a pit.*

1. In which lines does Chaucer show that the Jews were not liked by the Christians, and why?

2. Do you think that a false anti-Jewish story such as this has any value to a historian?

Medieval women

Unlike the Jews, women were not a small minority, but have often been seen as second class citizens in the medieval world. Just how true is this belief?

The great majority of people in medieval Britain, both men and women, lived as farmers. Surely this was a life dominated by men with the heavy physical work demanded in the fields? In fact, peasant life was very much about a partnership between husband and wife in raising a family and working the fields. At crucial times in the farming year, particularly harvesting, women worked alongside men in the fields. John Fitzherbert in his book *A Book of Husbandry* written in 1525 said of a farmer's wife's jobs:

> It is the wife's occupation to winnow corn, to make malt, to wash clothes, to make hay and to cut corn. In time of need, she should help her husband fill the dung-cart, drive the plough, go to market to sell butter, cheese, milk, eggs, chickens, pigs, geese and corn. And also to buy the things needed for the household, and to tell her husband truthfully what she has paid. And if the husband go to market to buy and sell, he should tell his wife in the same way. It they deceive each other, they are not likely to survive.

Women at work in the fields; from a manuscript produced around 1475

Single women would also work, taking jobs as dairymaids, for example, or as servants, or seasonal work in the fields. Married women did jobs to earn extra money such as baking and brewing of ale. Unlike beer, ale could not be stored for any period of time before spoiling, so had to be produced constantly. When beer became more available in the fourteenth century many an ale wife was put out of business. Women could also be found as small traders in local towns selling things like eggs and cheese.

In the town a women's life could closely resemble that of her country cousin, particularly as most townspeople kept animals and grew small gardens for food and there was a steady market for ale. There was also a greater demand for servants. Girls, before marriage, would become servants to learn about housekeeping, save money and even find a partner, for servants often married amongst themselves. Town life could offer even more opportunity for a few girls in gaining skills in trades such as silk making in London, although there weren't the same formal apprenticeships for girls as there were for boys.

Marriage was still what was expected of most women in towns and again they often formed an important partnership with their husbands, not only in managing their households but also in helping to run their craft or trade. The same guilds that stopped women from entering trades (see below, page 131) also included rules supporting the work of member's wives in the same trades. If widowed, these women sometimes took over the running of the craft or trade, either out of duty to their families or because it gave them the chance to show their independence.

One woman who tried to run a business on her own in the late fourteenth and early fifteenth centuries was Margery Kempe, who was later to become well known for her religious experiences. The daughter of the mayor of King's Lynn, Margery set herself up as a large scale ale-brewer after she married John Kempe. At one point, as she states in her book, *The Book of Margery Kempe*, she was 'one of the greatest brewers in the town'. But then her ales began to sour too soon, her servants left her and Margery had to close down her shop. Margery's story is unique in that it was written down, but she was certainly not alone among women in towns who attempted, sometimes very successfully, to run their own businesses.

Women of the highest classes at first glance seemed the least able to display much independence. Their value to their families was as a means to secure property and power through marriage alliances. These women may not have been given formal power, but there is plenty of evidence that, when married, they had a great influence on the lives of those around them. Sometimes, such as in the cases of Eleanor of Aquitaine and Isabella of France, they directed the politics of the time. Only Matilda, daughter of Henry I, tried to claim power in her own right rather than through marriage and she was, in the end, unsuccessful.

One highborn lady able to play an important role in politics of her time was Joan, an illegitimate half-sister of Henry III. She married Llywelyn the Great, Prince of Gwynedd, and worked hard to keep the peace between the Welsh and the English. In one of the letters she sent her royal brother, she wrote:

> *Know, lord, that I am grieved beyond measure that our enemies have succeeded in sowing discord between my husband and you. I grieve no less on account of you than on account of my husband, especially since I know what genuine fondness my husband used to have, and still has, for you, and how useless and dangerous it is for us, with due respect, to lose true friends and have enemies instead.*

High-born women spinning and weaving; from a manuscript produced around 1420

Joan proved successful during her lifetime in keeping the peace, and when she died in 1237 her husband built a Franciscan monastery over her grave.

Another woman who played a key role in her family's rise to power was Margaret Paston. The Pastons were an up-and-coming family in Norfolk who found themselves involved in a twenty-year struggle to claim an inheritance disputed by a number of others, to the point that Margaret had to write a letter asking her absent husband John for crossbows and poleaxes so that she could defend the family home from hostile neighbours. Several generations of Pastons produced letters, with Margaret being known to have written over a hundred. It is clear that John Paston depended upon his wife to look after his business while he was away trying to sort out the inheritance dispute. For example, in 1460 when Margaret's uncle John Berney died John sent a letter to ask his wife to:

> ...telle Thomas Holler that I and he be executours named. And therfore lete hym take heede that the goodes be kept saffe, and that no body knowe wher it shall lie but ye and Thomas Holler. [tell Thomas Holler that I and he are executors of the will. And therefore let him take care that John Berney's goods be kept safe, and that nobody know where they are except for you and Thomas Holler.]

Noble widows were by law granted a substantial wealth in land and money, sometimes to the anger of their sons who felt deprived of their inheritance. (In the earlier Middle Ages these widows had sometimes been forced by the Crown to remarry, leading to a clause in the Magna Carta to prevent this.) Some widows enjoyed this independence, others happily gave to their sons in exchange for being cared for and some retired to a nunnery.

The Church provided one of the few places in medieval Britain where a woman might rise by her ability into a position of authority as an abbess or prioress of a nunnery.

However, this gave chances to only a tiny minority. For most women of all classes their families and their marriages shaped their lives. A few might achieve real independence, but although most proved essential partners to their husbands they were never given a chance to stand on their own.

Exercise 7.6

Read the following source and then answer the questions:

SOURCE A: From a letter written by Hildegard of Bingen in 1147. Hildegard was a German abbess who experienced religious visions and preached on what she saw. This extract is taken from a letter she wrote to Father Bernard of Clairvaux.

> I beg you, Father, through the living God, to listen to me as I question you. I am greatly troubled by this vision which has appeared to me... I have never seen it with the outer eyes of the flesh. Wretched as I am (and more than wretched in being a woman) I have seen, ever since I was a child, great miracles, which my tongue could not utter had the Spirit of God not shown me them so that I might believe. Most true and gentle Father, answer in your goodness, your unworthy maidservant... Provide your servant-girl with comfort from your heart.

1. What do you think Hildegard means by 'I have never seen it with the outer eyes of the flesh'?

2. Hildegard was greatly respected by churchmen. What evidence is there in this extract that she didn't consider herself to be equal to men?

Exercise 7.7

1. Based on your knowledge so far, choose one area of medieval life (such as the nobility, religious orders, work or farming) and describe the role that women played in it.

2. Explain why there weren't as many opportunities for women as for men in the medieval period.

Medieval health and the Black Death

Death was a constant feature of existence in the medieval world. Poor diet, lack of medical knowledge and poor sanitation all played a part. You may associate blood-stained battlefields with this period in history, but only a tiny proportion of people died as a result of war.

Health and knowledge

There were doctors in the medieval world, but their understanding of the human body was very limited. There was little chance to study the human body as the Church had strict rules about the dead. It would certainly not have been lawful to cut up a dead body, for example. What limited knowledge there was relied on the works of ancient Greek and Roman doctors such as Galen, whose knowledge was based on treating wounded gladiators and dissecting pigs. Besides, surgery was seen as the job of the barber-surgeon, who one day might shave and cut hair, the next pull teeth and bleed patients.

Both the causes of, and cures for, illness were based on popular superstitions and religious beliefs. Since just about anyone could call himself a doctor, there was little chance for any real understanding of disease. Much was left to common sense and luck whilst many of the cures, such as bleeding, were often worse than the sickness itself. Bleeding involved cutting a patient in the hope that the ailment would come out of the body in the flow of blood. For the same reason, blood-sucking leeches were placed on the body in the hope that the leeches would suck the ailment out along with the blood. Illness was blamed on bad air, the position of the planets, or God's punishment for bad behaviour. Not surprisingly, the average life expectancy was low during the medieval period, certainly not above forty years. Children often died young and childbirth often resulted in the death of the mother. Poor sanitation in towns meant diseases spread easily.

A fascinating insight into early medieval medicine is found in the account of the Arab historian Usama ibn Mungidh (1095-1188), who reported how a 'doctor' treated his patients at Moinestre in the Holy Lands during the crusades:

> They took me to see a knight who had an abscess on his leg, and a woman with consumption. I applied a poultice to the leg, and the abscess opened and began to heal. I prescribed a cleansing and refreshing diet for the woman. Then there appeared a Frankish doctor, who said: "This man has no idea how to cure these people!"... He sent for a strong man and a sharp axe... The doctor supported the leg on a block of wood, and said to the man: "Strike a mighty blow, and cut cleanly!" And there, before my eyes, the fellow struck the knight one blow, and then another, for the first had not finished the job. The marrow spurted out of the leg, and the patient died instantly.
>
> Then the doctor examined the woman... "The devil has got into her brain," he pronounced. He took a razor and cut a cross on her head, then removed the brain so that the inside of the skull was laid bare. This he rubbed with salt, and the woman died instantly. At this point I asked whether they needed me, and as they didn't I left, having learnt things about medical methods that I never knew before.

Usama is clearly very scornful of the Christian doctor, and would certainly have considered him to be a butcher by the much higher standards of medical knowledge that existed in the East at this time.

A medieval doctor at work; from a 15th century manuscript

However, medieval people were not completely ignorant concerning health. For example, it was understood that poor drinking water could lead to illness, although there was no understanding of how bacteria in the water caused this. Most medieval people drank weak beer or ale with their meals, which was safer because water was boiled in the ale-making process, therefore killing the dangerous bacteria.

The Black Death and its spread

Against such a background, the spread of a plague known as the Black Death was a disaster waiting to happen. The Black Death, or Bubonic Plague, was a disease that started in Asia sometime in the early 1340s. It, and another even more dangerous form called Pneumonic Plague, spread rapidly westwards so that, by 1346, rumours of it began to reach Europe. At first, few people paid much attention since there were always stories of the strange happenings in the far off East. But, as stories continued to circulate about this plague, there was a general unease amongst Europeans.

A priest in what is now Belgium wrote what he had heard:

> In the East, hard by Greater India, in a certain province, horrors and unheard of tempests overwhelmed the whole province for the space of three days. On the first day, there was a rain of frogs, serpents, lizards, scorpions and many venomous beasts of that sort. On the second, thunder was heard, and lightning and sheets of fire fell upon the earth, mingled with hailstones of marvellous size; which slew almost all, from the greatest even to the least. On the third day, there fell fire from Heaven and stinking smoke, which slew all that were left of men and beasts, and burned up all the cities and towns in those parts.
>
> By these tempests the whole province was infected; and it is conjectured that, through the foul blast of wind that came from the South, the whole seashore and surrounding lands were infected...

Pneumonic Plague was spread through the air by infected people in the way that the common cold is, and attacked the lungs, causing a fever and spitting of blood that killed in two days. This version of the disease was not as common and seemed to appear largely in the winter.

Bubonic Plague, on the other hand, was caused by bacteria carried by fleas on the black rat. The fleas were infected by feeding on their host. The bacteria then multiplied in the fleas' stomachs, causing a blockage that led the fleas to starve. If one of these infected fleas jumped onto a human and attempted to feed, it spread the bacteria.

The symptoms of the Bubonic Plague began with the appearance of the **bubo**, a swelling of the lymph glands in the armpit or groin that could reach the size of an egg or small apple. Next, the victim would feel very sick and vomit, and develop dark blotches all over the body. The disease would then attack the nervous system, causing great pain. Five days after the buboes appeared, the victim usually died. For a very lucky few their buboes would burst and foul-smelling pus would discharge, showing that their bodies had successfully fought off the plague.

As Bubonic Plague spread to the Middle East, it infected the rats living on European trading ships. These ships then carried their cargoes to Italy, the centre of the European trade network. The first major Italian city to suffer was Florence, but soon the plague was spreading throughout Europe, reaching France and raging through Paris in the winter of 1348-1349. It was only a matter of time before the plague reached England.

Giovanni Boccaccio lived in Florence during the plague outbreak and wrote an eyewitness account of what he saw. Here are some of the things he wrote:

In Florence, despite all that human wisdom and forethought could think of to avert it, as the cleansing of the city from many impurities by officials appointed for the purpose, the refusal of entrance to all sick folk, and the adoption of many precautions for the preservation of health; despite also humble prayers addressed to God, often repeated in both public procession and otherwise by the devout; towards the beginning of the spring... the doleful effects of the plague began to be horribly apparent...

Victims of the plague; from a manuscript produced around 1360

Some people reacted by deciding to '*shun and abhor all contact with the sick and all that belonged to them.*' Other people '*maintained that to drink freely, to frequent places of public resort, and to take their pleasure with song and revel... was the best remedy for so great an evil.*' Still others, trying to take a middle way, '*walked carrying in their hands flowers or fragrant herbs... which they frequently raised to their noses... because the air seemed to be everywhere laden and reeking with the stench emitted by the dead and dying and the odours of drugs.*' Still others simply left everything and fled the city.

The Black Death in Britain

In June 1348, the Bubonic Plague reached the town of Melcombe in Dorset when two ships arrived carrying the disease. Very shortly afterwards, Southampton and Bristol became infected and the disease began to spread rapidly.

As Geoffrey le Baker, an Oxfordshire cleric living at that time, wrote:

At first it carried off almost all the inhabitants of the seaports in Dorset, and then those living inland, and from there it raged so dreadfully through Devon and Somerset as far as Bristol, and then men of Gloucester refused those of Bristol entrance to their country, everyone thinking that the breath of those who lived amongst people who died of plague was infectious. But at last it attacked Gloucester, yea and Oxford and London, and finally the whole of England so violently that scarcely one in ten of either sex was left alive.

As in the rest of Europe, no-one understood what was causing this plague that killed old and young, rich and poor alike. It is not known exactly how many people died, but most historians believe at least one third of England's population died between 1348 and 1349. In London, with a population of 70 000, about 30 000 people died. Cleaning the streets, lighting fires to clear the air, using flowers or sweet herbs to purify the air, avoiding the sick; none of this had any effect. All sorts of strange and wonderful cures were tried, such as cutting open buboes, or even placing a frog on a bubo to absorb the poison, again to no avail.

The Church suffered greatly during the plague. Many priests tried to look after the members of their church by visiting and tending the sick and so died of the disease themselves. Three Archbishops of Canterbury died in quick succession. Monasteries were also hard hit; in St. Albans, the first man to die was the abbot and forty-seven monks soon followed. In spite of constant prayer, the disease did not stop, leading to a group called **flagellants** appearing in England. They believed that by whipping themselves and drawing blood that they would pay penance for man's sins so that the disease would stop. As with everything else, this failed and, because of it many people lost respect for the Church.

In the countryside, the plague sometimes wiped out whole villages. As villagers died, the fields and animals were left unattended. In their search for causes, some villagers accused women of witchcraft and killed them.

In both town and country, there were too many bodies for proper burials and often the priest was either dead or had run away. Pits and trenches were hurriedly dug and the dead were dumped in with little ceremony. As nobody really kept count of the numbers, the surviving writers tended to exaggerate how many people had died, which helped increase the feelings of doom and panic. So great was the immediate impact of the Bubonic Plague that it stopped the fighting of the Hundred Years' War in France for several years. In the north of Britain, the Scots thought they saw an opportunity to strike at the English whilst the country seemed to be dying of the plague. But the Scottish army was infected by the disease and its soldiers fled, helping to spread the plague throughout Scotland. As Geoffrey le Baker wrote:

> While this great calamity was devastating England, the Scots, rejoicing, thought that they would obtain all they wished against the English… But sorrow following on the heels of joy, the sword of the anger of God departing from the English drove the Scots to frenzy… In the following year it ravaged the Welsh; and at last, setting sail, so to speak, for Ireland, it laid low the English living there in great numbers.

A new world

As the survivors of the plague began to look about them in 1350, they found that their world had changed. In the countryside, where there had been too many mouths to feed and not enough work, suddenly there were many cottages empty and fields unploughed. The lords of the land were desperate to find labourers to plough and tend the crops and so many offered much higher wages to their workers. Once busy town streets now grew weeds and many a craftsman's shop was closed. This meant that prices for goods made by the surviving craftsmen went up.

There were attempts to turn back the clock and make the peasants live and work the way they had before 1348. Parliament, made up of the lords who were suffering because of the changes, passed the **Statute of Labourers** in 1351, a law that stated that peasants had to accept the wages and conditions of work that applied before 1348. Any peasant found breaking this law would be jailed. Any lord who was tempted to offer higher wages would be fined. However, although some people were punished under this law, the lack of manpower forced many lords to break the law and offer higher wages and better conditions. In order to keep earning money for their family, many peasant women found that they had to work longer hours and take on tasks that previously only the men had done, such as carpentry and ironmongery.

So, did the Black Death destroy England? A huge number of people died and many more died later on, because the Bubonic Plague was to return again and again over the next three hundred years. Some villages were eventually abandoned because of such great loss of life. There was certainly plenty of misery, as every family in the land was touched in some way by this disease. Towns struggled to survive as did monasteries and nunneries. Prices of many things, including food, did go up. Many of the old ways were threatened and lost.

On the other hand, the changes brought a better world for some. There was the opportunity for many peasants to create a better life for themselves, with better pay and working conditions. Because of the loss of so many priests, English soon became the language of teaching and the shortage of educated men helped lead to the creation of new colleges to train more scholars.

Problems caused by the changes brought on by the Bubonic Plague were to play a major part in events in England for some time. This is particularly evident in the outbreak of the Peasants' Revolt in 1381 (see page 123).

Exercise 7.8

Write out the following paragraphs, filling in the blanks using information from the chapter.

In the medieval world doctors depended upon the work of ancient _____ and _____ doctors such as _____. Surgery was the job of the _____- _____. Sickness was blamed on _____, the _____ of _____ or _____ _____.

The Black Death came from _____. It had two forms, _____ and _____. The first major European city to suffer was _____ in the country of _____. It reached England in _____, first infecting the port town of _____ in _____.

Exercise 7.9

Either draw a cartoon showing how people caught the Bubonic Plague or write a paragraph explaining it. Can you find the name of the bacteria that caused the disease?

Exercise 7.10

Write a few sentences about each of the following:

1. Symptoms of Bubonic Plague

2. Symptoms of Pneumonic Plague

3. Ways medieval people tried to avoid the plague

4. Ways medieval people tried to cure the plague

5. Flagellants

Exercise 7.11

Re-read the account written by Boccaccio on page 118 and answer the following questions.

1. In the first paragraph, what steps were taken in Florence to try to prevent the plague? In your answer, use quotations when possible.

2. In the second paragraph, name two different ways that people in Florence dealt with the coming of the plague. Again, try to use quotations in your answer.

3. Think about who wrote this source, when he wrote it and what he wrote. Do you think that this source offers accurate information about how Europeans reacted to the plague? Explain your answer.

Exercise 7.12

Read the accounts of Geoffrey le Baker and Boccaccio on page 118.

1. What steps did the men of Gloucester take to try to prevent the plague entering their city?

2. How did people think that the plague spread, according to Geoffrey?

3. How is Geoffrey's account similar to that of Boccaccio and how is it different? Quote from both passages in support of your answer.

Exercise 7.13

Write the story of how people in England in 1348 tried to deal with the arrival of the Black Death. Start with a sentence or two saying how the disease arrived, then write a paragraph about what people of the time believed was causing the disease. In the next paragraph, write about the different ways that people tried to prevent or cure the disease. In a final sentence or two, write about how effective these various ideas and cures were in stopping the disease.

Exercise 7.14

1. Make a chart with the title 'The Consequences of the Black Death'. Then make two sub-headings, 'Good Things' and 'Bad Things'. Using the information on pages 116-119, fill in the chart. Are all the consequences easy to fit into the two lists?

2. Here is a chance to show some of your judgement about the Black Death. Write a short four-paragraph essay about the consequences of the Black Death, starting with an introduction, then two 'content' paragraphs, one looking at bad things, one looking at good things, and finally a concluding paragraph stating what you think was the most important consequence.

Chapter 8 Richard II and life in the towns

Richard II, 1377-1399

Richard II, like his great, great, great-grandfather Henry III, became King when he was very young. He was unfortunately more like his great-grandfather Edward II in the way his reign ended.

The Peasants' Revolt

At the age of fourteen, and still very much under the care and protection of men such as his uncle John of Gaunt, Richard faced one of the greatest challenges of his reign. The Peasants' Revolt of 1381 shook the very foundations of English life and brought the young King into real danger.

Some of the causes of the revolt lay in the events of the past. As we have seen, the Black Death had changed English life in many ways, including the way in which the land was farmed. Labourers demanded higher wages and villeins wanted to be paid for their work on their lord's land. This was made worse in some places where some villeins were allowed to rent their land like freemen and others were not.

Richard II; a contemporary portrait

Added to this, some lords used the law courts to have their own way and to keep wages low, based on the Statute of Labourers of 1351.

Jean Froissart, a French priest who knew many of the nobles of England, wrote the following about the causes of the revolt:

> In England, as in other countries, the noblemen have great power over the common people. Their villeins plough their lords' lands, gather and bring home their corn, make their hay, cut their wood and bring it home. These unhappy people began to complain. They said that in the beginning of the world there were no bondmen, and so no one ought to be bond now. They were men, like their lords, so why should they be kept under, like beasts? This, they said, they would no longer suffer. If they did any work for their lords, they would have wages, the same as any other.

There was also a general unhappiness about the war against France, which had been going badly by the end of Edward III's reign. Some in England were also questioning the way the Roman Catholic Church worked. One priest in particular, John Ball, had caused enough problems to be put in prison.

The trigger for the uprising was the **Poll Tax**. In order to raise money for the French war, the government demanded that everyone pay a tax. This tax was first used in 1377 and again in 1379, but in 1381 everyone over the age of fourteen was expected to pay one shilling, three times more than the previous rate. This wasn't a problem for the wealthy, but was almost impossible for the poor. When very little money was collected, the government tried to get tough with some areas of the country and this sparked off the uprising, which first broke out at Brentwood in Essex.

In late May and early June 1381, an armed uprising of peasants and townspeople occurred over the south-east of England and in particular Essex and Kent. Law officials and tax collectors were attacked and some were killed. Rochester Castle and Canterbury were captured. John Ball, the 'mad' priest, was released from prison and became one of the leaders. He is believed to have said to the rebels: 'When Adam delved and Eve span, who then was the gentleman?' In other words, why should peasants do all the hard work while the lords did nothing? Another leader to appear was Wat Tyler. These men and others led the rebels to London to see the King and to demand changes.

There was panic in London as the rebels approached and the city leaders tried to close the gates. But there were people in the city who agreed with the rebels and they helped them enter on 13th June. Prisons were broken open and certain places were burnt, such as the Inns of Law and John of Gaunt's Savoy Palace (though any rebel trying to steal from the burning palace was quickly punished by the others). A number of foreigners, particularly the Flemish, were killed as they were seen as a threat to the jobs of ordinary Londoners.

At the time, the young King Richard was in the Tower of London with his advisors. He had made one attempt to talk to some of the rebels from a boat on the Thames before they entered the city, but had failed. According to a contemporary chronicle, the *Anonimalle Chronicle* written by an unknown author:

> From a turret in the Tower, the King could see the Savoy and many other buildings all on fire. He called his lords to his room and asked them what he should do. None of them could give him any advice. Wherefore the King said that he would have it cried that all men should go the next morning to Mile End. There he would meet them to listen to their demands. He did this so that the rebels would leave the Tower and go to Mile End. Those in the Tower could then escape.

The next day King Richard rode to Mile End, just outside the city, to meet the rebels. He agreed to the rebel demands, that there be no more villeins, wages should be fair and that no one would be punished for the rebellion. This satisfied a large number of the rebels who immediately started for home. But others were not satisfied and some of these rebels managed to break into the Tower of London and seize two important government officials, Simon of Sudbury (who was both Chancellor and Archbishop of Canterbury) and Robert de Hales (the King's Treasurer), who were hauled off to Tower Hill and beheaded. Sudbury's head with his mitre hat nailed on was paraded on a pole through the streets.

The death of Wat Tyler; from a manuscript produced around 1460

Once again the boy King agreed to meet the rebels, this time at Smithfield on Saturday 15th June. Wat Tyler presented a number of radical demands, such as all lordships to be abolished except for the King, and for Church lands to be seized. Again Richard agreed. What happened next is not clear. This is how the *Anonimalle Chronicle* recorded the event:

Presently, Wat Tyler called for a jar of water. When it was brought, he rinsed his mouth in a very rude and disgusting fashion before the King. Then he made them bring him a jar of ale, of which he drank a very great deal.

At this time, a gentleman from Kent asked to see the rebel leader. When Tyler was pointed out, the gentleman said he was the greatest thief and robber in all Kent. For these words Tyler tried to run him through with his dagger. But the Mayor of London, William Walworth, accused Tyler of contempt and violence in the presence of the King, and arrested him. Tyler struck the Mayor in the stomach with his dagger. But, as God would have it, the Mayor was wearing armour, and took no hurt. Then the mayor drew his sword and gave Tyler a deep cut in the neck, and another on the head. In the fight, one of the King's gentlemen drew his sword and ran Tyler through the body, mortally wounding him.

Before the surprised rebels could react, Richard rode to them and shouted out that he was their leader and they should follow him. This caused a number of the rebels to leave. Soon, a number of armed men appeared from London and the rest of the rebels were surrounded and forced to depart.

There were smaller risings throughout the country in June, but by the end of the month, the King's forces were in control. The promises made by Richard were not kept and many of the leaders of the rebellion, including John Ball, were found and hanged.

Did the Peasants' Revolt achieve anything? Villeins continued to work for their lords, for as Richard told one group: 'Villeins ye are, and villeins ye shall remain.' But changes in population and farming meant the old system was dying, if more slowly than many peasants wished. England's nobility became much more careful when dealing with the commoners. One thing was certain: the Poll Tax was never used again in the Middle Ages.

The fall of Richard II

Richard, partly because of his success during the Peasants' Revolt, became convinced of his own powers and was not happy being under the control of his uncle, John of Gaunt. Thus he wrote:

I am of full age to govern my house, and my household, and also my realm. For it seems unjust to me that the condition I am now in should be worse than the condition of the least of my kingdom.

Richard wanted to create a stronger monarchy by increasing his own powers, but he and his supporters in government ran into trouble with some of the mightiest lords of the land and Parliament. To put a check on the King, the Merciless Parliament was called in 1388. It demanded the arrest and trial of a number of Richard's government officials, including the Chancellor Sir Michael de la Pole. Most fled the country but the vice-chamberlain Sir Simon Burley was executed. A group of nobles called the **Lords Appellant**, which comprised the Duke of Gloucester and the Earls of Arundel, Warwick, Nottingham and Derby, took control of the government and ran the country for a year before handing power back to the King in 1389. Things settled down for several years, as Richard seemed to have learned his lesson and a truce was agreed with France.

However, Richard never really forgave the Lords Appellant for the way he felt he had been mistreated. He quietly continued to increase his power by creating his own permanent force of knights and archers, starting peacetime taxation, making himself more 'royal' by being addressed as 'Your Majesty' and making anybody he glanced at bow before him. In 1397, Richard struck at his enemies by arresting three of the Lords Appellant and executing one, exiling one and having one murdered. The other two Lords Appellant, including his first cousin Henry Bolingbroke, son of John of Gaunt, had joined with Richard, but he distrusted them and a quarrel between them allowed the King to send both into exile.

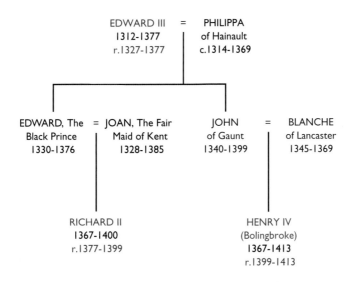

The relationship between John of Gaunt, Richard II and Henry Bolingbroke

Richard now had an obedient country, where he seemed to reign supreme. However, the death of his uncle, John of Gaunt, in February 1399 upset everything. Richard seized Gaunt's lands for himself instead of allowing Henry Bolingbroke to inherit his father's vast estates. Enraged, Bolingbroke broke his exile and returned to England and won support from important nobles. Richard had been in Ireland and returned to be arrested by Bolingbroke. There did not seem to be many in England ready to stand up for the King and he was deposed in Parliament in September 1399. Henry Bolingbroke now became King Henry IV. Richard was imprisoned at Pontefract Castle and was murdered in February 1400.

Exercise 8.1

Match the following events with their correct dates and put them into the proper chronological (time) order:

1.	Wat Tyler is killed at Smithfield.	(a)	1397
2.	Death of John of Gaunt.	(b)	February 1400
3.	The Merciless Parliament is called.	(c)	February 1399
4.	Sudbury and de Hales are killed.	(d)	15th June 1381
5.	Poll Tax is introduced.	(e)	1388
6.	Richard II is murdered.	(f)	14th June 1381
7.	King Richard II is deposed by Parliament.	(g)	13th June 1381
8.	The Lords Appellant hand power back to Richard.	(h)	September 1399
9.	The rebels enter London.	(i)	1377
10.	The Lords Appellant are arrested.	(j)	1389

Exercise 8.2

Write a sentence or two about each of the following:

1. The Poll Tax

2. John of Gaunt

3. Wat Tyler

4. The Merciless Parliament

5. The Lords Appellant

Exercise 8.3

Look at the *Anonimalle Chronicle* description of the death of Wat Tyler on page 124 and compare it to the picture on page 125. Then answer the following questions:

1. According to the *Anonimalle Chronicle*, what did Tyler try to do to the Mayor of London? Make sure you use a quotation when answering this question.

2. Does the picture of the death of Tyler agree or disagree with the *Anonimalle Chronicle's* account? Make sure you clearly compare what the two sources show or say before giving your final answer.

Exercise 8.4

Copy this picture of Richard II and complete the table. On one side of the picture write Richard's good points as a king, on the other the bad. Did Richard deserve to be deposed?

Exercise 8.5

Re-read pages 123-126 on the Peasants' Revolt.

(a) Describe the part played in the Peasants' Revolt by Wat Tyler.

(b) Explain why Richard was finally able to defeat the rebels.

Richard II

Good points	Bad points

Life in the towns

Nearly everybody in the medieval world lived and worked in the countryside. Still, slowly over this period towns did grow and some new towns were planned and built. So what would life have been like in one of these small but busy places?

What did towns look like?

Towns were built to take advantage of the ways that people travelled. All were on major roads and many were next to rivers that needed to be crossed and might also have boat traffic. Many of these towns had walls surrounding them and some also had a defending castle; London had two. The walls were not just for defence, they also helped the town control who came in and out, and to take **tolls** (taxes) from those bringing goods into the town. Once inside the walls a visitor would be struck by the noise and the smell of so many people in such a small space. The streets were not paved, so in bad weather mud was a constant problem. Buildings were made largely of **wattle and daub**, a method of construction that used a wooden frame for the structure, and woven branches and twigs covered with plaster to fill in the walls. These houses would often have thatched roofs and would be crowded into the streets, although in many towns there would be open spaces behind this line of buildings that could be reached by a back lane. Because of these spaces, cattle, sheep, pigs and chickens could be kept within the town walls. In most towns there would be at least one open area used as a market place, where stalls could be set up to sell local produce.

Amidst all the bustle of town life stood the churches. A town of any size would have a number of churches, usually built of stone and acting as centres of town life. The city of London had over a hundred churches, along with St Paul's Cathedral. In addition, there were other religious buildings such as monasteries, nunneries and hospitals. One of the many sounds of town life would have been the frequent ringing of church bells.

What did people do in towns?

Many travellers would come to a local town to buy things that they could not make for

An artist's impression of a medieval town house

themselves. This could range from fine cloth and costumes to pottery and ironware. There was also the opportunity to purchase goods from overseas, particularly in port towns. Different crafts tended to group together in larger towns, so that you might find a whole street of goldsmiths, for example, or of leather-workers. Butchers helped create some of the worst smells in a town if they were not made to clean up their waste. In London, the street where they worked was called Stinking Lane.

Towns housed both the very poor and the very rich. Beggars were common, as there was a much better chance of **alms** (money given to the poor) with so many people crowded together. The wealthiest merchants would also be there, for their riches came from trade and they would want to live near their warehouses and businesses. In between would be the vast majority of the population, from day labourers (hauling goods to and from the warehouses and shops) to servants, craftsmen, stallholders and all the other people who would live in a town. One very noticeable group would be the **apprentices**, boys who had been bound by their families with an agreement called an **indenture** to learn a trade. A **master craftsman** would take on one or more apprentices to teach them his trade in exchange for their labour and a sum of money. The apprenticeship might take seven years or more, during which time the master was to feed, clothe and take care of his charges. In bigger towns, large groups of apprentices could often be found at the centre of trouble and the young lads would certainly enjoy the entertainments a town had to offer. After their apprenticeship had been served, the young men would become **journeymen** and be paid by their master for their work. The final step for an apprentice was to become a master himself, though this was difficult to achieve.

The guilds

In many towns the craftsmen gathered together to form a **guild**. This was an organisation intended to protect them and their crafts. In larger towns and cities, different trades and crafts each formed their own guilds. Each guild had a set of rules for its members to follow, setting out who could work in their craft, how apprentices were to be trained and making sure the goods made by members of the guild were of a good quality. But guilds did more than this; a guild might support a particular church, and it would help the widows and families of its members and look after the sick. The most important men of the guilds would also have a role to play in town government, even having the chance to become **mayor**, or leading citizen, of the town or city. In the later medieval

A medieval craftsman and his helpers; from a 15th century painting by Jean Bourdichon

period, some guilds became wealthy enough to build **guildhalls** for themselves. Guilds were also involved with other apsects of town life, such as providing **pageants**, spectacular processions, and **mystery** or **miracle plays**, which both entertained, and in the case of the plays, gave religious instruction. The guild system also sometimes allowed women a chance to take on a role other than housekeeping and childbearing. In some cases, when a craftsman died, his wife would take on the business, something not possible for those farming on the manors. In Paris, we know that the women had over a hundred different types of job, and many became wealthy this way. This might not have been so common in England, and certainly some guilds actively discouraged women from being involved.

An example of the way a guild would look after its members can be found in records of medieval London. Here is how the tawyers', or leather tanners', guild worked:

> We will find a wax candle to burn before Our Lady [the Virgin Mary] in the Church of All Hallows, London Wall. Also, each person of the trade shall, from time to time, put in the box such sum of money as he shall think fit.

> If one of the trade shall become poor, whether through old age, or because he cannot work, he shall have every week from the said box seven pence. After his death, if he have a wife who is a good woman, she shall have weekly seven pence from the box, so long as she shall behave herself and not marry.

Dishonest traders and craftsmen were also dealt with by the guilds. Here are some more examples from London's records.

> 1) It was shown that John Penrose sold red wine that was bad and unwholesome for man, in deceit of the common people, and in contempt of our Lord the King and to the shameful disgrace of the City.

> It was ordered that the said John should drink a cup of the same wine that he sold to the common people; and that the rest of such wine should then be poured over the head of the same John; and that he should no longer follow the calling of vintner [someone who sells wine] in the City of London, unless he can win a pardon from our Lord the King.

> 2) Robert Porter, servant of John Gibbe, baker, was brought before the Mayor and Aldermen [members of the town council]. It was said that when the Mayor went into Cheap Street to assay [test] the bread, he, knowing that the bread of his master was not of full weight, took a penny loaf and in it pushed a piece of iron, intending to make the loaf weigh more.

*When questioned, the same Robert admitted the offence. For his
falsity and deceit it was ordered that he should be put in the
pillory* for one hour, with the said loaf and piece of iron hung
around his neck.*

* A **pillory** was a form of punishment where the legs of the guilty person were
locked in place. The **stocks** followed the same idea, but locked both legs and arms,
and sometimes even the head, in place. The offender would be jeered at and
humiliated by the public.

Using the stocks; from a 15th century German painting

Town government

The earliest towns in England were the property of their lords, just like any other land. This meant that the lord had the right to demand labour and taxes from the townspeople. Over the medieval period, a number of towns succeeded in having this changed by being granted a **charter** by either their lord or the king. This legal document gave the town the right to have its own government, its own laws and taxes. Kings such as Richard I and John were happy to grant charters as they received a payment for doing so. The great merchants and leaders of guilds became the men who would then rule the town as aldermen and mayors. Because of this independence, a villein or serf who had run away from his manor and reached a town could earn his freedom if he stayed there for a year and a day.

The dangers of town life

Town life offered many chances for a decent life for medieval people, but there were also dangers. Buildings tended to be crammed together as the population grew, so there was a greater risk of fire. Some crafts, such as pottery and metalworking, were often placed on the fringes of a town for just this reason. However, as every household needed an open hearth for both cooking and heating, fires were a common hazard.

Crime was also a danger. With large numbers of people living closely together there were always problems with **cut-purses** (pickpockets) and other petty criminals, so keys and locks were a necessary part of town life. There were no police forces, but

watchmen would patrol at night and some towns had a **curfew**, a time when everybody was expected to be indoors. If a criminal was discovered, the '**hue and cry**' was raised and everyone helped to chase after him.

One major problem in town life was dealing with rubbish and waste. Clean water, sewers and efficient drainage were almost non-existent. As towns began to pave their streets, a drainage channel would be made in the centre, and often streets were deliberately built running down a hill to allow rubbish to be washed away. Conditions were excellent, however, for the spread of disease. The outbreak of the Bubonic Plague in the fourteenth century was a disaster for Britain's towns (see page 116) and, in places like London, death was so common that the population was only kept stable or growing by the arrival of a steady stream of newcomers.

Exercise 8.6

Match the two halves of the following sentences:

1. Most town houses   (a) were made of stone.

2. Some of the worst smells in a town   (b) were made of wattle and daub.

3. Boys who were trained in a trade   (c) were made by butchers.

4. Charters   (d) were legal documents allowing town government.

5. Some important buildings like churches   (e) were known as apprentices.

6. When the 'hue and cry' was raised,   (f) provide mystery plays.
    everyone had to

7. One thing a guild did was to   (g) chase the criminal.

Exercise 8.7

Write several sentences about each of the following:

1. The growth of towns

2. Guilds

3. Apprentices

4. Crime in towns

5. Disease in towns

Exercise 8.8

What would it be like walking through the streets of a medieval town? Either draw a picture of a street scene, trying to use as much of the information in this chapter as you can, or write a paragraph describing what you might see, hear and smell.

Exercise 8.9

Look at the sources about dishonest traders on page 132 and the picture below, then answer the questions.

1. How is the baker being punished in the picture?

2. Look at both sources about dishonest traders on page 132. How does the picture agree with the written sources?

To answer this make sure you clearly write about what each of the written sources says, using quotations. Compare these to what the picture shows and then make a clear statement about how the picture does or does not agree with each written source.

A baker punished for breaking the rules of the guild; from a 14th century manuscript. Notice the loaf tied around the baker's neck

Chapter 9 The three Henrys

Henry IV; from a 17th century portrait

Henry IV, 1399-1413

As a young man, Henry Bolingbroke had been admired for his **chivalry**. Chivalry was the mixture of courage and consideration that all knights and lords aspired to, that is, hoped to achieve. He had been a crusader and a **pilgrim** to the Holy Land. But the eldest son of John of Gaunt, chivalrous or not, was going to need all his ability in order to survive as King of England.

Henry's claim to the throne was weak and there was at least one other person, the Earl of March, with a better claim. There is also no doubt that the way Henry took the throne from Richard II was illegal, even though Parliament was used to support his coronation.

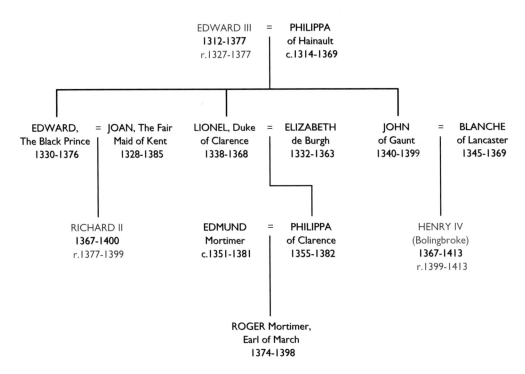

The relationship between the Earl of March, Richard II and Henry Bolingbroke

The first years of Henry's reign were to be full of troubles, both at home and overseas. Many of the Welsh had never been happy with their conquest by Edward III. Under the leadership of Owain Glyndwr, who proclaimed himself the true Prince of Wales, a rebellion broke out and the rebels seized many of the key English castles in Wales. At the same time, Henry had problems with the Scots. The French also attempted to take advantage of the situation and attacked English holdings in Gascony and Calais. In 1403, the Percy family, led by the Earl of Northumberland and his son, Henry 'Hotspur', rebelled and tried to place the young Earl of March on the throne. They made an alliance with Glyndwr, but Henry IV moved faster and more effectively than they expected. The King joined with his son Henry, Prince of Wales and caught Hotspur and his army at Shrewsbury, where Hotspur was killed and the rebels were defeated. Northumberland continued to make trouble for several more years but eventually he too was killed in battle.

Unlike Richard II, Henry was willing to work with Parliament, even when some of its members criticised his rule. Money was a big problem, both for the continuing fighting and because Henry proved poor at controlling how much he spent on his court. The King had to accept royal councillors working with Parliament to control his money. The councillors did help with the money matters and helped the government carry on as Henry fell ill.

The Battle of Shrewsbury, 21st July 1403; from a 19th century children's history book

When Henry IV died in 1413, he left a country far more settled than when he had become King. The Welsh rebellion had been all but crushed, the situation with Scotland was stable and the French had become involved in a civil war that England was already trying to use for its own advantage. At first, people accepted Henry's son's right to take over the throne, but the way Henry IV, first of the so-called Lancastrian kings, had taken the English crown was to bring great problems in the years ahead.

Exercise 9.1
Copy the paragraph below, filling in the blanks:

Henry IV became King in _____ by overthrowing King _____.
Because of the way he had become King, _____ had problems holding on to
his crown. The Welsh under _____ rebelled, while to the north the
_____ were causing problems. In 1403 the _____ family rose in
revolt, but Henry '_____' was defeated at the Battle of _____.

Henry IV also had money problems and _____ forced him to allow councillors
to control his finances. At his death the matter of how the _____ kings had
obtained the throne was to cause problems in the years ahead.

Exercise 9.2
Write an **obituary** for Henry IV. Make sure you mention how he became King and
how he dealt with the problems he faced. Was he was right or wrong in what he did?

Henry V, 1413-1422
Henry V's short reign has left him with a
reputation as a warrior king in the same
mould as Richard I and Edward III.
Before he died at the age of thirty-five
Henry had not only won a famous
victory against great odds in France, but
he had also seized all of Normandy and
had established his right to be King of
France.

The young King was very serious and
made sure that money was more wisely
spent than it had been under his father.
This was very important, as it appears
that, quite early in his rule, Henry
decided that he wanted to reclaim large
sections of France for England.

Henry V; from a 15th century portrait

War in France
After a careful build-up of supplies and money, Henry V landed in Normandy in
August 1415, seizing the port of Harfleur, then marching on a *chevauchée* north to

Calais. A *chevauchée* is a hit-and-run raid often practised by the English during the Hundred Years' War. It was not meant to take land, but to weaken the enemy and gather plunder. These raids caused untold misery to the French people in their path.

Henry V was attempting to take advantage of civil war in France to try to reclaim his French lands. The King of France, Charles VI, was mentally ill and this left two sides, the Burgundians and the Armagnacs, fighting to gain control. Both sides tried to enlist Henry's support, allowing the English King to play one side off against the other.

Henry's landing at Harfleur caught the French by surprise. The English besieged the town but found its defences too strong to take quickly. Cannons were eventually used to break down the walls but, before the port town surrendered in late September, Henry's army had been greatly reduced by dysentery. English plans for a *chevauchée* deep into France had to be cancelled, but Henry insisted on a march of 160 miles from Harfleur to Calais, apparently not expecting any resistance.

The Armagnacs, however, had gathered a large army and, with the help of the Burgundians (with whom they had patched up relations in the face of the threat from the English) intended to destroy the invading English. When Henry's men tried to cross the River Somme, they found the crossings blocked by French troops. Henry was forced to march east until he found two unguarded fords to cross. For several days, the English continued to march towards Calais in the rain, only to find their way blocked by the French on the evening of 24th October. This is what happened, according to the *Gesta Henrici Quinti*, written by an unknown writer (thought to have been a priest in Henry's court):

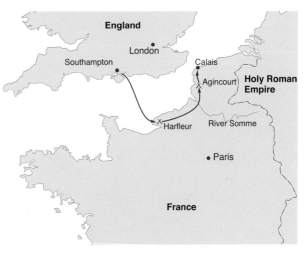

Henry V's French campaign of 1415

> We crossed over the river as quickly as possible but, just as we reached the top of the hill, we saw the grim-looking ranks of the French. They were in compact masses, their numbers being very much greater than our own. At length, they took up a position facing us. They filled a huge field like a swarm of locusts, and there was only a small valley between us and them.

That night the exhausted English, with little food and sleeping in the rain, waited for daylight and battle. They were outnumbered, having 7000 archers and fewer than a thousand men-at-arms, against a French force of at least 12 000. Some historians have said that the English had as few as 6000 men, and the French as many as 60 000. Other accounts at the time say that Henry sent word to the French that he would return Harfleur and pay for damages if he and his army were allowed to continue to Calais. If he did make this offer, clearly it was refused.

The Battle of Agincourt, 1415

The English army that awaited the French attack on the morning of 25th October depended upon its archers armed with the longbow. Three groups, or **battles**, of men-at-arms and knights were commanded by the King in the centre, the Duke of York on the right and Lord Camoys on the left. Groups of archers were probably placed in the gaps between the battles whilst the majority of archers were massed at each end of the line and angled forward, so as to be able to fire upon any French knights attacking the centre of the line. The archers drove pointed stakes in front of them to help protect them from a French cavalry charge. The English stood in a muddy ploughed field with woods on either side that would force the French to attack straight towards them. Henry made a speech telling his men of his right to lands in France and warning his archers that the French had promised to cut off the three fingers of their right hands if they were captured.

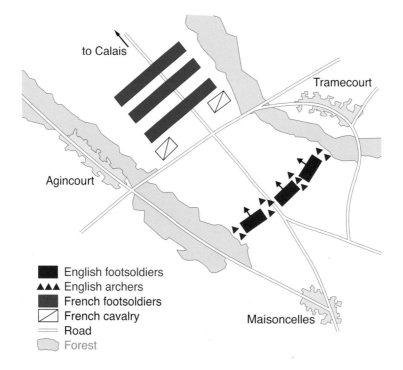

The Battle of Agincourt, 25th October 1415

The French army, commanded by Marshal Boucicaut and the Constable d'Albret, were waiting for further reinforcements, and had no intention of throwing themselves at the English archers. The *Gesta Henrici Quinti* stated:

> The number of them was terrifying. They placed squadrons of cavalry, many hundreds strong, on each flank of their vanguard. And that vanguard was drawn from all their nobles and the pick of their forces. With its forest of spears, and the great number of helmets gleaming, it was, I would guess, thirty times more than all our men put together.

For several hours, the two armies stood in sight of each other. Finally, Henry ordered his army to advance until they were 300 yards from the enemy. The English were now at the narrowest point of the battlefield, strengthening their defensive line between the woods. Each archer quickly planted the six-foot stake he carried in the ground in front of him, and began to unleash a storm of arrows. Unlike at Crécy, the French men-at-arms in 1415 wore plate armour, which was not only solid steel but curved, so that at least some of the longbow arrows would have glanced off. But the mounted men on the wings suffered as the arrows struck their horses and they tried to charge the archers, churning up the soil but failing to achieve anything.

The first line of dismounted French knights then began to advance and the narrowness of the battlefield forced them ever closer together. Their plate armour proved heavy and cumbersome in the clinging mud. Even so, under a constant shower of arrows, the French attack at first drove the English centre back. Henry ordered his archers, who wore no armour, to drop their bows and attack the struggling French. As the *Gesta Henrici Quinti* said:

> When their arrows were all used up, they seized axes, stakes, swords and spearheads that were lying about. With these, they struck down, hacked and stabbed the enemy.

The archers moved quickly amongst the French men-at-arms, stabbing through armour joints or pushing the armoured men into the mud. Some drowned when others fell on top of them.

Into this confusion the second French line advanced, also bunched together and disorganised. They had to climb over piles of bodies to reach the English line. Their leader, the Duke of Alençon, actually beat Henry down to his knees but was then overwhelmed. Soon the second attack was finished, leaving piles of dead and wounded Frenchmen lying higher than a man's head. The French nobles and knights who were still alive were taken to the rear as captives for ransom; the rest were killed where they lay. At this stage, Henry suddenly received a report that his rearguard and baggage were under attack, so he ordered that the captives be put to death. His men

The Battle of Agincourt, from a 19th century children's history book

were reluctant to do this because of the rich ransoms the prisoners could bring. Nonetheless, a large number of prisoners were butchered, including one group burnt alive in a hut, before it became obvious that the battle was over. The final French line, horrified at what had happened to the first two lines, rode off. After four hours of battle, Henry V had won an astonishing victory.

The next day, the English army, possibly having lost as few as 300 men in the battle, marched on to Calais with 1500 prisoners. On the battlefield they left the bodies of many French nobles and knights; altogether French losses were about 10 000 men.

How do we know?

Historians agree that the number of Frenchmen who lost their lives at Agincourt was huge compared to English losses. But historians do not agree on how many English soldiers were killed and wounded. This is largely because the contemporary sources do not agree with each other and nobody at the time kept an accurate record. So, a military historian writing in 1976 can state that a few died and several hundred were wounded, whilst another book, a dictionary of battles, puts English losses at about 400. A book written in 2005 specifically about Agincourt states that at least 112 men can be identified as killed in the battle, but that records are incomplete and this does not include the wounded who died later. All this just goes to show that, as historians, we may never know for sure what happened in the past. Our job is to find out as much as we can, using all the available evidence.

The aftermath of Agincourt

Henry's real successes came several years later when he led another expedition to Normandy and proceeded to take all the important towns. The temporary alliance between the Burgundians and the Armagnacs was at an end, and the Burgundians, because of the murder of the Duke of Burgundy by the Armagnacs, had allied themselves with Henry and seized Paris, holding Charles VI captive. Philip, the new Duke of Burgundy, agreed with Henry in 1420 to the Treaty of Troyes, by which Henry married Catherine of Valois, daughter of Charles VI, and was to inherit the French throne after Charles VI's death. Henry appeared to have in his grasp the goal of his great-grandfather Edward III: to be the King of England and France. While involved in further campaigning in France, however, Henry contracted dysentery which eventually killed him at the height of his power in 1422. He left a nine-month-old son Henry as the ruler of England, and when Charles VI died just two months later, this child also became King of France.

Would Henry V have succeeded as King of England and France? The Dauphin, Charles VI's last remaining son, was leading the Armagnac forces that held most of southern France and he was not ready to surrender. Henry had done so well because France was split by civil war. Once the Armagnacs and Burgundians agreed to join together, it was unlikely that the English would have been able to hold on to the lands they had taken, much less keep the French crown. How long would the English people have been willing to continue to pay for war? There were signs, by 1422, that some were beginning to question the heavy taxes and it is likely that Henry would have soon run into trouble with Parliament.

Henry V and the Lollards

Famous for his victories in France, Henry V is also remembered for his attacks on those at home who challenged the authority of the established Church. Chief among these were the **Lollards**. The Lollard movement was first founded in England by John Wycliffe during the reign of Richard II. To the Lollards, the Bible was the only true source of the Christian religion. However, the Bible was only available in Latin, and so the Lollards had English translations drawn up so that the people could understand it. These translations were illegal. They also questioned the power of the Roman Catholic clergy and some even questioned the power of the Pope. Henry V, like his father before him, executed these believers by burning them at the stake, the punishment for those whose beliefs were considered to be **heresy**, and dangerous to the established Church.

Exercise 9.3

Match the two halves of the following sentences:

1. The English were so successful in France because they	(a) allied with the English.
2. The Burgundians were important to Henry V because they	(b) took control of Normandy.
3. Henry V is best known because he	(c) became next in line to the French throne after the death of Charles VI.
4. The greatest success the English had was when they	(d) faced the French while they were divided by civil war.
5. By the Treaty of Troyes, Henry V	(e) won the Battle of Agincourt.

Exercise 9.4

Write a sentence or two about each of the following:

1. Owain Glyn Dwr

2. Lollards

3. Charles VI

4. The Duke of Burgundy

5. The Treaty of Troyes

Exercise 9.5

Read the following sources about the Battle of Agincourt and then answer the questions:

SOURCE A: From the *Gesta Henrici Quinti*

> *A shout went up that the enemy's mounted rearguard was about to make an attack on us. We were few and weary; they were a great many, and still fresh. Immediately, the prisoners were killed, either by their captors, or by others. This was to prevent them turning on us in the fighting that was about to happen.*

SOURCE B: From *Agincourt* by Juliet Barker, published in 2005.

> *Was there any real need to kill the prisoners at all? Some historians, following the monk of St. Denis, have claimed that there was no genuine threat of a renewed French attack,*

and that the whole terrible episode was based on a panicked response to a false alarm. Ghillebert de Lannoy, on the other hand, thought it was a rally by Antoine, Duke of Brabant, that prompted the order.

1. Look at Source A. Why were the prisoners killed?

2. Look at Source B. Does it support Source A? Does it have information that agrees with Source A and does it have information that disagrees? Make sure you explain your answer.

3. Look at both sources. Which would be more useful for understanding why the French prisoners were killed?

When answering this question, make sure you look at the provenance of each source, including who wrote it, when it was written, why it was written, what it says and where it was written. Not all of these questions can be answered or are important for every source, but together these questions should always be used to judge a source's usefulness.

Exercise 9.6
Write an essay about why Henry V won the Battle of Agincourt. In your introduction, state where the battle was fought and who won. In your next few paragraphs, look at why Henry V was marching north and how his army was caught by the French, how the two sides compared, how the battle was fought and the reasons that Henry V's army won. In your conclusion, briefly summarise your main points and explain what you think was the main reason that Henry V won the battle.

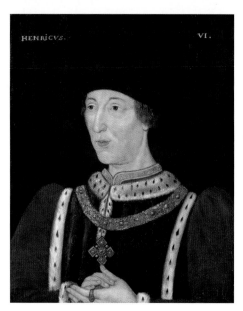
HENRICVS.   VI.

Henry VI; from a 16th century portrait

Henry VI, 1422-1461

Henry's son Henry VI was King only in name for the first fifteen years of his reign until he reached the age of sixteen. Governing England and France on his behalf was a royal council supported by Parliament. The most important leaders of this council were Henry's two uncles, the Dukes of Bedford and Gloucester.

For some time, the Duke of Bedford managed to hold on to, and even increase, English lands in France with the help of Burgundy. But when English forces moved to besiege and take the city of Orléans, the tide began to turn against them, helped by the efforts of a girl named Joan of Arc.

Joan of Arc

Joan started life as a peasant girl in the countryside of France. She believed that God was speaking to her and telling her to act to save France from the English. Although the English boy-king Henry VI was now King of France as well as King of England, many French people still looked to Charles VI's son, the Dauphin, to be their ruler.

In 1428, Joan managed to convince a local lord to take her to see the Dauphin, who called himself Charles VII, although he had never been properly crowned. Apparently, Charles tried to test her by having someone else pose as the Dauphin while he stood with the rest of the court. Joan ignored the impostor and bowed before the real Dauphin. Whether this story is true or not, Charles seems to have been convinced that Joan could offer some help to his cause and gave her armour, a horse and a banner, then sent her to join with an army marching to save Orléans. Joan was not a great war-leader but seems to have inspired the French soldiers to fight better. The English army was driven off and the French army began to seize English strongholds. When a small English army tried to save one of the strongholds, they were surprised by the French whom Joan urged on with the words: 'You have spurs, so use them!' The English were defeated and several English commanders were captured.

Joan convinced Charles to march to Reims, the town where French kings were supposed to be crowned, but which was now held by the English. Reims was quickly taken and Charles was properly crowned King of France with Joan standing near him holding her banner. Many of the French believed that God was now on their side and that they were fighting a holy war against the English and Burgundians.

But Joan soon began to lose her reputation for being unbeatable. The French attempt to take Paris failed and Joan was wounded in the thigh in one of the attacks. Joan did have some further limited success but was then captured by a Burgundian soldier during a raid. She was handed over to the English and taken to their main base, the Norman city of Rouen. Joan was accused of being a witch, partly because she wore men's clothing, and she was treated very roughly. The English believed they had to destroy Joan because she threatened their belief that God supported their claims in France. Joan was found guilty of witchcraft and heresy and sentenced to be burnt at the stake. This was done at the market place in Rouen on 30th May 1431. Joan was just nineteen years old when she died.

Joan of Arc, from a 19th century children's history book

Despite the help she had given him, Charles VII made no attempt to try to save Joan. Perhaps he, like many in his court, was jealous of her power. Over twenty years later, however, he ordered a new trial in Rouen for Joan which found her innocent and helped convince the Pope to grant her a full pardon. Joan of Arc had helped the French believe in their cause once more.

Henry VI takes control

When Henry reached sixteen, he appeared to be ready to rule. The third Lancastrian king was intelligent, good-looking, very religious and interested in education, founding both Eton College and King's College, Cambridge. However, unlike his father, Henry was not interested in war, and he was to be the first King of England not to lead an army into battle. He was also easily influenced and unable to deal responsibly with money. In a world where military ability was highly valued and the nobility was ready to take advantage of a weak king, Henry VI was not suited to rule.

Henry tried to bring the fighting in France to an end. Even though he married a French princess, Margaret of Anjou, and managed to arrange a two-year truce, the French were now united under Charles VII and ready to drive the English out. With the Duke of Bedford dead, a lack of money and strong reluctance amongst the English to admit defeat, trouble was brewing for Henry. The French had created a much more professional army and proceeded to sweep the English armies and garrisons away in Normandy until, by 1450, the only areas left in English hands were Gascony and Calais.

Meanwhile, in England, a group of nobles surrounding the King was accused of misusing its position. This group, led by the Duke of Suffolk and the Queen, deliberately kept Henry away from Parliament and another key noble, Richard, Duke of York, who was the heir to the throne until the birth of Henry's son Edward in October 1453.

In 1450, a rebellion broke out in Kent led by Jack Cade. This was a reaction to the loss of Normandy and the poor government England had been suffering. What triggered the revolt was the rumour that the King planned to punish the people of Kent for the murder of his favourite, the Duke of Suffolk, after Parliament had forced his exile. When faced with royal troops at Blackheath near London, the rebels had retreated, but when the King was forced by his own troops to dismiss some of the nobles who surrounded him, the rebels took new heart. On the evening of 3rd July, they entered London. Henry had fled. The rebels demanded that Henry's 'evil' councillors be punished and the government be reformed, including bringing the Duke of York into power. In spite of Cade's attempts at discipline, the rebels looted and burned parts of London, dragged Lord Saye out from the Tower and killed him. After three days of violence, Londoners fought back by preventing the rebels from re-entering the city at London Bridge in an all-night battle. Promises were made concerning reform and some rebels returned home. Jack Cade was hunted down, wounded and died before being tried for treason. But outbreaks of revolt were to continue in the south-east of England for the next few years.

Instead of York, Edmund Beaufort, the Duke of Somerset, became the key man behind the King. For a short time things improved, for although Gascony was lost to Charles VII, some of the towns were briefly retaken by the English. Money matters also seemed to be improving and the Parliament of 1453 was happy to grant taxes. Then in the summer of 1453, Henry VI suddenly had a mental collapse; he did not respond to people talking to him and could no longer look after himself.

The coming of civil war

With Henry VI's mental collapse, Richard, Duke of York, stepped in as protector. For eighteen months Richard ruled in Henry's name. He had Somerset arrested and placed in the Tower, and Queen Margaret's attempts to have more control were rejected. But when Henry recovered in 1455, York was once again cast out and Somerset was put back in power. Both men had become more interested in protecting their own power than serving king or country. When a great council was called in 1455, the Yorkist nobles feared they would be arrested. They gathered 3000 men and marched south to meet the King and Somerset with 2000 men at St. Albans on 22nd May. There was an attempt at talking, but soon the Yorkists attacked and fought their way into the centre of the town. Somerset and other key Lancastrian lords were killed and Henry VI was taken by force into the control of Richard, Duke of York.

Henry, who had never really recovered from his first mental illness, was rapidly becoming the puppet of the two sides, each determined to control the government of England. Civil war did not actually break out until 1459, but the reasons for it already existed. The King was incapable of ruling the country and his Queen became an important leader. Queen Margaret was the daughter of the Duke of Anjou and the niece of Charles VII. She had married Henry when he was twenty-three and she was fifteen. She had been brought up in Italy and was considered both learned and beautiful. As her husband became feeble Margaret attempted to take more control, putting her followers into key government positions. She was a determined enemy of Richard, Duke of York, and her actions in the late 1450s helped drive the country closer to civil war. When fighting finally broke out, Margaret was to prove a key leader for the Lancastrian side.

Exercise 9.7

Match the following statements with their dates and write them out in chronological order:

1.	Somerset is killed at the Battle of St. Albans.	(a)	October 1453
2.	Henry VI becomes King of England.	(b)	1455
3.	Joan of Arc is burnt at the stake.	(c)	1449
4.	Henry VI's son Edward is born.	(d)	22nd May 1455
5.	Richard, Duke of York, becomes protector.	(e)	Summer 1453
6.	Henry VI suffers a mental collapse.	(f)	March 1454
7.	Jack Cade's rebellion.	(g)	1428
8.	Henry VI recovers from mental illness.	(h)	1422
9.	Henry VI marries Margaret of Anjou.	(i)	30th May 1431
10.	English forces are defeated at Orléans.	(j)	1450

Exercise 9.8

Write a sentence or two about each of the following:

1. Richard, Duke of York
2. Jack Cade
3. Edmund Beaufort
4. The Battle of St. Albans
5. Queen Margaret

Exercise 9.9

Write the story of one of the three Henrys. In your introduction, say why you chose this Henry. In your content paragraphs, write first about his life, then about the most important things that he did. Finish with a conclusion that briefly summarises his life and achievements, and say why you think he is important.

Chapter 10 The Wars of the Roses

The Wars of the Roses are famous for having torn the English nobility in half and for ushering in a new royal dynasty, that of the Tudors. So what were these wars, who fought them, and why?

The first war

In 1459, with King Henry VI totally incapable of ruling, the followers of the Duke of York prepared for the worst as Queen Margaret organised both her forces and a Parliament to declare York and his supporters traitors. The Lancastrian nobles heavily outnumbered the Yorkists, but the Yorkist lords were the most powerful and wealthy nobles in England and several were very capable military commanders. Each of the great lords involved in the Wars of the Roses had a number of symbols that they could use on banners and their supporters could wear on their clothing. One such symbol for Richard of York was the white rose, whilst one symbol of the Lancastrians was the red rose. This is why historians later named these civil wars the Wars of the Roses.

The outlawed Yorkists bided their time and then attacked from Calais and Dublin.

Yorkists or Lancastrians pick white or red roses; from a children's history book published in 1905

They seized London and captured Henry VI, now reduced to a puppet king. However, when Richard, Duke of York seemed ready to have himself declared king, even his own followers hesitated. As a result, York and Henry VI agreed to a compromise called the **Act of Accord**. This said that Henry would remain King but that the throne should then pass to the Duke of York, rather than to the King's seven-year-old son Edward.

Queen Margaret had no intention of allowing this deal to stand. She continued to raise troops in the north of England. When the Duke of York marched with an army against the Lancastrians, he was surprised at the Battle of Wakefield and killed.

The Lancastrian cause now seemed on the verge of victory as the Queen's men marched south, defeating the Yorkist Richard Neville, Earl of Warwick, at St. Albans and recapturing Henry VI.

At this crucial moment, two factors denied the Lancastrians victory. First, the people of London refused to open the gates of the city to Margaret. Second, the Duke of York's eldest son Edward, claiming the crown for himself, marched from the West Country with an army that he joined with that of Richard Neville, the Earl of Warwick. The Lancastrians withdrew north, allowing Edward and Warwick to enter London.

The Yorkists, having lost control over Henry VI, now declared that Edward was the rightful king of England, and crowned him Edward IV. Edward then led his army northwards after the Lancastrians, finally tracking them down at Towton on 29th March 1461. In a blinding snowstorm, the two sides fought a vicious battle that lasted most of the day. Eventually, the Lancastrian line collapsed and many Lancastrian soldiers were cut down as they tried to flee. While Queen Margaret, Henry VI and the young Prince Edward managed to escape to Scotland, around 8000 Lancastrians died, as well as 5000 Yorkists, making Towton one of the bloodiest battles fought on English soil. It also established Edward IV firmly as King.

The Wars of the Roses, 1455-1485

Wars of the Roses (part one)

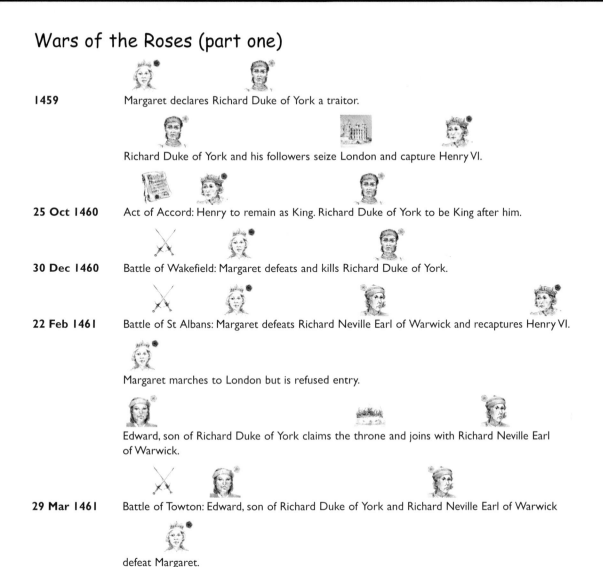

1459   Margaret declares Richard Duke of York a traitor.

Richard Duke of York and his followers seize London and capture Henry VI.

25 Oct 1460   Act of Accord: Henry to remain as King. Richard Duke of York to be King after him.

30 Dec 1460   Battle of Wakefield: Margaret defeats and kills Richard Duke of York.

22 Feb 1461   Battle of St Albans: Margaret defeats Richard Neville Earl of Warwick and recaptures Henry VI.

Margaret marches to London but is refused entry.

Edward, son of Richard Duke of York claims the throne and joins with Richard Neville Earl of Warwick.

29 Mar 1461   Battle of Towton: Edward, son of Richard Duke of York and Richard Neville Earl of Warwick

defeat Margaret.

Edward IV, 1461-1483

Edward IV; from a 15th century portrait

The new King had proved himself a very good military commander, but he soon realised that he needed to be more than that to be a good king. With so many nobles supporting the Lancastrians, Edward was highly dependent upon a few Yorkist lords and especially Richard Neville, Earl of Warwick. Warwick is often called the 'Kingmaker' in history books. He played a very important role in the earlier part of the Wars of the Roses. A nephew of Richard of York, he and his family became key supporters of the Yorkist side, although Warwick himself did not prove to be a particularly good military commander. However, when Edward IV secretly married Elizabeth Woodville and brought many of her relations to court, and then followed the Woodvilles' advice concerning a treaty with Burgundy, Warwick was greatly upset. In 1469, fearing that his influence was being undermined, Warwick joined up with Edward's brother George, Duke of Clarence, and invaded England from Calais. Edward IV was defeated by the pair and briefly captured, but soon escaped and forced Warwick to flee to France. There, Warwick switched sides once more, and this time joined with Queen Margaret and the ousted Henry VI in a bid to seize power. They invaded England in 1470 and Edward IV was forced to flee the country.

The second war

It was not long before Edward returned, managed to raise an army and was joined by his brother the Duke of Clarence, who had himself changed sides. Edward reached London before facing Warwick on Easter Sunday 1471 at Barnet, north of London. There, in a thick fog, Warwick was defeated and killed as he tried to escape. Edward followed this up by tracking down Queen Margaret and Prince Edward's army as it tried to reach Wales, defeating it at Tewkesbury. The young Prince Edward, the son of Henry VI, was killed. Edward IV's position was further strengthened on his return to London in May 1471 when Henry VI, once again a prisoner, died in the Tower of London.

With both Henry VI and his young son now dead, Edward IV continued to rule unopposed for another twelve years and began rebuilding the position of the Crown that had been so badly damaged during Henry VI's reign. Edward still needed the support of key lords and indeed proved so generous to his supporters that several, including his brother Richard, Duke of Gloucester, became very powerful. His other brother, George, Duke of Clarence, proved too untrustworthy and was executed for treason in 1478. One story is that he was drowned in a barrel of Malmsey wine. When Edward died in April 1483, he left a twelve-year-old heir, Edward, in the centre of a power struggle that would lead to the final stage of the Wars of the Roses.

Wars of the Roses (part two)

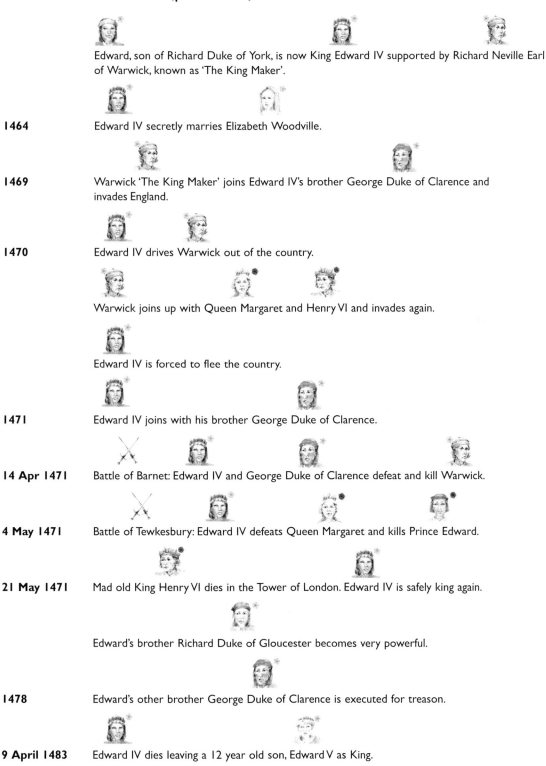

Edward, son of Richard Duke of York, is now King Edward IV supported by Richard Neville Earl of Warwick, known as 'The King Maker'.

1464 Edward IV secretly marries Elizabeth Woodville.

1469 Warwick 'The King Maker' joins Edward IV's brother George Duke of Clarence and invades England.

1470 Edward IV drives Warwick out of the country.

Warwick joins up with Queen Margaret and Henry VI and invades again.

Edward IV is forced to flee the country.

1471 Edward IV joins with his brother George Duke of Clarence.

14 Apr 1471 Battle of Barnet: Edward IV and George Duke of Clarence defeat and kill Warwick.

4 May 1471 Battle of Tewkesbury: Edward IV defeats Queen Margaret and kills Prince Edward.

21 May 1471 Mad old King Henry VI dies in the Tower of London. Edward IV is safely king again.

Edward's brother Richard Duke of Gloucester becomes very powerful.

1478 Edward's other brother George Duke of Clarence is executed for treason.

9 April 1483 Edward IV dies leaving a 12 year old son, Edward V as King.

Exercise 10.1

Match the two halves of the following sentences:

1. The Lancastrians   (a) was killed at the Battle of Tewkesbury in 1471.

2. The Act of Accord   (b) outnumbered the Yorkists during the Wars of the Roses.

3. Richard, Duke of York   (c) was killed at the Battle of Wakefield in 1460.

4. The Battle of Towton   (d) stated that Richard of York was to be king after Henry VI.

5. Richard Neville   (e) was the bloodiest battle of the Wars of the Roses.

6. Prince Edward   (f) fought for both sides in the Wars of the Roses.

7. Henry VI   (g) was killed in the Battle of Barnet in 1471.

8. The Earl of Warwick   (h) was murdered in the Tower of London.

Exercise 10.2

Write a sentence or two about each of the following:

1. Queen Margaret

2. Elizabeth Woodville

3. The Earl of Warwick

4. Richard, Duke of Gloucester

5. George, Duke of Clarence

Richard III, 1483-1485

At the death of Edward IV, both his widow's family, the Woodvilles, and Edward's brother Richard, the Duke of Gloucester, took steps to seize control of the young heir Edward V. It was Richard that proved the more ruthless and successful by executing his opponents and placing both the young King Edward V and his younger brother Prince Richard in the Tower of London, at that time both a royal palace and a prison. Up to this point, Richard's actions might be seen as those of a loyal and concerned uncle trying to protect both his nephews and himself against potential enemies. Some of his methods, however, such as the execution of Lord Hastings, a

Richard III; from a 16th century portrait

loyal supporter of his brother Edward IV and an ally against the Woodvilles, were ruthless. And when the time came for the young Edward V to be crowned in July 1483, Richard suddenly took the throne for himself, declaring that the boys were not legitimate, and proclaiming himself King Richard III. Soon afterwards the two boys disappeared.

There continues to be much debate about what happened to the 'Princes in the Tower'. Stories have been told of both princes, or at least the younger, Prince Richard, being sent away and it is possible that one or both of them were still alive in the reign of Henry VIII. However, most historians believe that the two boys were murdered, and the majority place the blame on Richard III. He had already proved that he was capable of taking ruthless action and the boys stood in the way of his claim to the throne. Some years later Polydore Vergil, an Italian scholar who arrived in England during Henry VII's reign and was encouraged to write a history by Henry, wrote the following about the princes' fate:

> Richard determined by death to despatch his nephews because so long as they lived he could never be out of danger; therefore he sent orders to Robert Brackenbury, Lieutenant of the Tower, to procure their death by some convenient means… When Richard understood the lieutenant to make delay of that which he had commanded, he committed the charge of hastening the slaughter unto James Tyrell who, being forced to do the King's commandment, rode sorrowfully to London, and, to the worst example that has almost ever been heard, murdered those babes of the royal issue.

> This end had Prince Edward and Richard his brother; but with what kind of death these children were executed is not certainly known.

Sir Thomas More, writing at the time of Henry VIII, also blamed Richard III and Tyrell:

> Sir James Tyrell devised that they should be murdered in their bed, to the execution whereof he appointed Miles Forest; to him he joined one John Dighton. Then, all the

others being removed from them, this Miles Forest and John Dighton about midnight came into the chamber and suddenly lapped them up among the clothes, and so bewrapped them and entangled them, keeping down by force the featherbed and pillows hard unto their mouths, that they gave up to God their innocent souls into the joys of Heaven, leaving to the tormentors their bodies dead in the bed.

The Princes in the Tower, from a children's history book published in 1905

There is very little solid evidence about the fate of the princes; only hearsay from the time and accounts written later by men who wished to blacken Richard's name. Sir Thomas More's account above has often been accepted as accurate although it was based on a supposed confession Tyrell made, of which there is absolutely no record. As More later served as Chancellor to Henry VIII, a King who (as we will see) would have been very keen to blacken the name of Richard III, there is no doubt that his account is questionable. Other more contemporary writers only report rumours of the boys' deaths. But if we accept that most English people during Richard III's rule believed that Richard had had the princes put to death, this would certainly explain his lack of popularity before the Battle of Bosworth.

The Battle of Bosworth, 1485

Richard III had little chance to show his qualities as King. He was very popular in the north of England, where he held most of his lands, but the southern nobles were not very sure of him. One of his main supporters, the Duke of Buckingham, raised a revolt against him and, although the King crushed this and executed the Duke in November 1483, he became even more dependent upon his northern supporters. Another great blow to Richard was the death of his only son, Edward, in 1484, soon followed by the death of his wife.

Meanwhile, Richard faced a threat in the form of Henry Tudor, Earl of Richmond, who was in exile in France. Henry held a tenuous claim to the throne through his mother, representing the illegitimate Beaufort line of Edward III's son John, and he was waiting for his chance to invade. He took his chance in August 1485, landing near Milford Haven in Wales with a small French army and marching into England. Gathering support on the way, he found Richard III waiting for him near Market Bosworth in Leicestershire.

The Battle of Bosworth, fought on 22nd August 1485, was a crucial moment in the Wars of the Roses, although it did not end them. All indications were that Richard III, with his larger army in its superior position on Ambion Hill, should easily have defeated Henry Tudor's army. But even though Richard's army outnumbered Henry's, the King could not totally trust his commanders, particularly Northumberland, who commanded his rear division. There was also the matter of the Stanleys. Lord Thomas Stanley and his brother Sir William Stanley were both suspect with good reason. Lord Stanley was married to Margaret Beaufort, who was the mother of Henry Tudor through her previous marriage with Edmund Tudor, Earl of Richmond. But Lord Thomas's son, Lord Strange, was being held as a hostage by Richard, so when the armies met at Bosworth the Stanley forces, perhaps 3000 strong, stood to the side overlooking the two armies and awaited developments.

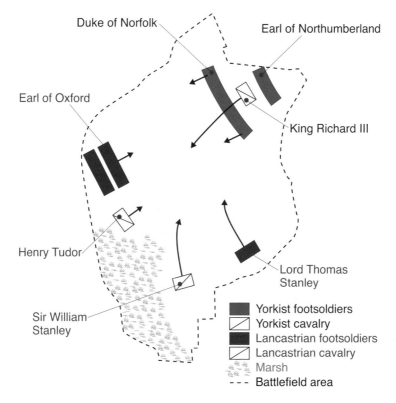

The Battle of Bosworth, 22nd August 1485

Henry Tudor's army of around 5000 men marched around a marsh at the foot of Ambion Hill before its front battle (see page 159), under the Earl of Oxford, turned to face Richard's forces. After firing a barrage of longbow arrows, the Duke of Norfolk led Richard's front battle down the hill and a vicious struggle began. The main weapon of many of the soldiers was the bill, a sharp-edged weapon set on a staff or pole that could cut, stab and hook an opponent. Mixed in with these soldiers would be the dismounted men-at-arms and knights, many of whom would be wearing plate armour. To defeat an enemy wearing full plate armour was difficult as blades and arrowheads would simply slide off the angled metal protection, so heavy, battering weapons were often used.

From the top of the hill, Richard III watched the battle ebb and flow. More men were fed into the fight on both sides but still the Stanleys stood and watched. What was clear was that Henry Tudor expected the Stanleys to join him as he had left his army weak nearest to them. Richard decided to lead his mounted reserve of knights and men-at-arms towards that flank, perhaps having spotted the banners of Henry Tudor. Some accounts state that Richard deliberately charged at the group of men around Henry hoping to reach his opponent and kill him. He certainly killed the man carrying Henry's personal banner. It was at this point that the Stanleys belatedly moved and attacked Richard's troops. Meanwhile, Northumberland's battle stayed on the hill and did nothing to help the Yorkist king. In the midst of the fighting Richard's horse was killed and he went down fighting, battered to death by some of the Welsh soldiers fighting for the Tudor cause. Polydore Vergil later wrote:

> Henry bore the brunt of the fighting longer than even his own soldiers would have thought, who were now almost out of hope of victory, when, behold, William Stanley and 3000 men came to the rescue; then truly in a very moment the residue all fled, and King Richard was killed manfully in the thickest press of his enemies.

The Yorkist army fled in disorder whilst Lord Stanley greeted his stepson Henry Tudor, the new King Henry VII. There is a story that the crown that Richard III had been wearing on his helmet had fallen off during the fighting and had landed on a hawthorn bush. It was recovered and Lord Stanley placed it upon Henry's head. The body of Richard was taken, naked, to Leicester where it was buried.

Henry VII, 1485-1509

For much of his reign, Henry VII's claim to the throne was shaky and he had to work hard to keep the crown. He had won because the surviving Lancastrians, as well as some unhappy Yorkists, had supported him. There was also the issue of the 'Princes in the Tower', the two sons of Edward IV, whose deaths could not be confirmed. One clever move Henry made was to marry Elizabeth, daughter of Edward IV and sister of the two princes, but he waited to have her crowned as Queen until he was surer of his position. A king who had taken the throne by force was an easy target to lose his crown by force.

Henry VII; from a 16th century portrait

The first really serious test of Henry VII's right to rule came within two years and was masterminded by Margaret of Burgundy, Edward IV's sister. A young man named Lambert Simnel was pretending to be Edward, Earl of Warwick, while the real Warwick was locked up in the Tower of London. Simnel landed in Ireland, was declared the true King of England and gathered support, including 2000 men sent by Margaret. The Earl of Lincoln joined him and led the invading force that landed in England in June 1487. Henry VII, however, was well prepared and led his own army to meet the Yorkists at Stoke near the town of Newark on 16th June. The battle was bloodier than Bosworth but, once again, Henry's army won and the Earl of Lincoln was killed. Lambert Simnel was captured and Henry showed him mercy, giving him a job in the royal kitchens. Following the battle Henry VII finally had his wife Elizabeth crowned as Queen, for he was now much surer of his hold on the throne.

Many historians believe that the Battle of Stoke finally finished the Wars of the Roses. However, the plots against Henry were not finished. Margaret of Burgundy, still a nuisance to the King, played a key role in the most dangerous, that of Perkin Warbeck. Warbeck, who was born in Tournai (now in Belgium), arrived in 1491 in Ireland, where a group of Yorkists convinced him to pretend to be Richard, Duke of York, the younger of the two 'Princes in the Tower'. He then arrived in Burgundy, where Margaret declared he was indeed her nephew, and began plotting an invasion of England. Henry became aware of this threat through his spies and discovered that members of his own household were involved, including Sir William Stanley, who had come to his aid at the Battle of Bosworth. Stanley was tried and executed, and Henry VII then had his three-year-old son Henry made Duke of York to counter Yorkist claims. An attempted invasion of England failed in 1495, so Warbeck and his men sailed on to Ireland to join rebels there. When this too failed, he and his supporters arrived in Scotland to ask for aid. At first, this proved successful and Warbeck was even allowed to marry an important noble's daughter. But Henry took decisive action and forced the Scots to back down, even though he had to fight off a rebellion from the West Country at the same time. Warbeck then joined these rebels in the West Country but Henry's army soon defeated them too, and Warbeck was captured. At first, Henry showed mercy and made Warbeck, like Simnel, part of his household. However, Warbeck tried to escape and ended up in the Tower. Finally, in 1499, the key Yorkist plotters in Ireland were captured and they, along with Warbeck and Edward, Earl of Warwick, were put on trial. Perkin Warbeck was hanged on 23rd November 1499 and the poor Earl of Warwick, whose only real crime was to be alive, and thus be a threat to the Tudor claim to the throne, was executed on 28th November.

As the year 1500 began, Henry VII could really begin to believe that, after fifteen years, his hold on the crown of England was secure. If all those who had wished him ill had managed to unite in 1497, he might very well have lost his throne; but he had survived.

Exercise 10.3

Match the following events with their dates and put them into the correct chronological (time) order:

1. The Battle of Stoke.   (a) 1495

2. Edward IV dies.   (b) 22nd August 1485

3. The execution of Perkin Warbeck.   (c) November 1483

4. The Battle of Bosworth.   (d) April 1483

5. The execution of the Duke of Buckingham.   (e) 28th November 1499

6. Richard seizes the throne.   (f) July 1483

7. Perkin Warbeck attempts to invade England.   (g) 16th June 1487

8. The execution of Edward, Earl of Warwick.   (h) 23rd November 1499

Exercise 10.4
Write a sentence or two about each of the following:

1.   Margaret of Burgundy

2.   Lambert Simnel

3.   The Earl of Lincoln

4.   The Battle of Stoke

5.   The Earl of Warwick

Exercise 10.5
Look at the two contemporary sources on page 157 concerning the murder of the two princes in the Tower and answer the questions that follow:

1.   According to Polydore Vergil, why did Richard III want the two boys killed?

2.   According to Sir Thomas More, who actually carried out the murders?

3.   Using specific examples from the sources, show one way in which Polydore Vergil and Sir Thomas More agreed about the boys' murder and one way in which they disagreed.

4.   How much can you trust what each of these sources tells you about the death of the two princes? You need to consider who wrote each source, when they wrote it, why they wrote it, how much is fact or opinion, and where they got their information.

Exercise 10.6
Write a description of the Battle of Bosworth. In your description, talk about the two armies that fought, the events of the battle and who won in the end.

Exercise 10.7
Write an essay describing how Richard III lost his throne. Start with an introduction that briefly states how you know that Richard III failed. Then look at the problems he faced when becoming King, how he tried to deal with his problems and why he failed at the Battle of Bosworth. Finish with a brief summary of Richard's efforts and your conclusion about how well he did as a King.

Exercise 10.8

Write an essay describing how Henry VII held on to his throne. Start with an introduction that briefly states why you think Henry succeeded. Then look at his problems when he became King, what steps he took to deal with rebellion and why, by 1500, his throne was secure. In your conclusion, briefly summarise how he dealt with his problems and state how well you think he did as a king.

Appendix 1: Timeline

The monarchs of England, 1066-1500

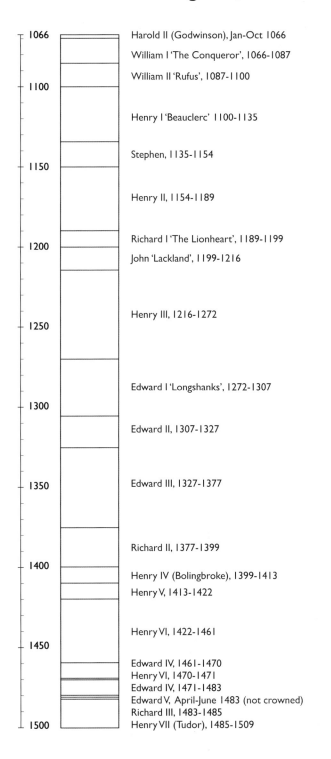

1066	Harold II (Godwinson), Jan-Oct 1066
	William I 'The Conqueror', 1066-1087
	William II 'Rufus', 1087-1100
1100	
	Henry I 'Beauclerc' 1100-1135
1150	Stephen, 1135-1154
	Henry II, 1154-1189
1200	Richard I 'The Lionheart', 1189-1199
	John 'Lackland', 1199-1216
1250	Henry III, 1216-1272
1300	Edward I 'Longshanks', 1272-1307
	Edward II, 1307-1327
1350	Edward III, 1327-1377
1400	Richard II, 1377-1399
	Henry IV (Bolingbroke), 1399-1413
	Henry V, 1413-1422
1450	Henry VI, 1422-1461
	Edward IV, 1461-1470
	Henry VI, 1470-1471
	Edward IV, 1471-1483
	Edward V, April-June 1483 (not crowned)
	Richard III, 1483-1485
1500	Henry VII (Tudor), 1485-1509

Appendix 2: Family trees

Chapters 1-2

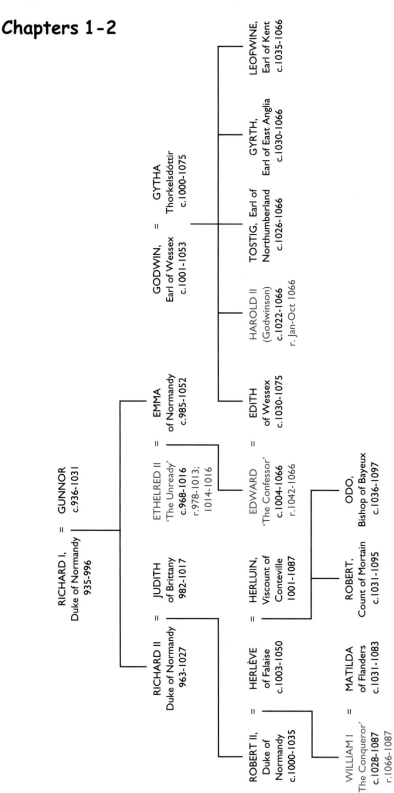

Chapters 3-5

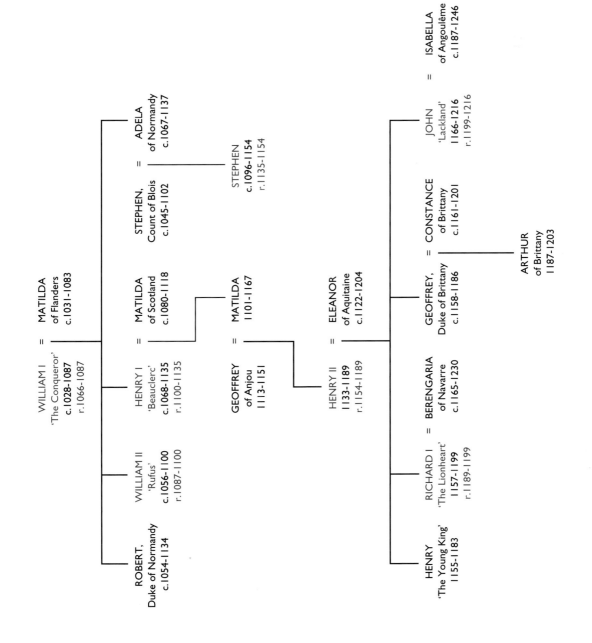

Chapter 6

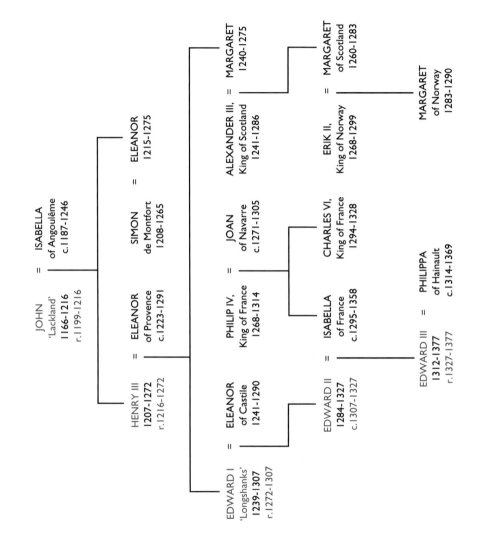

Chapters 8-10

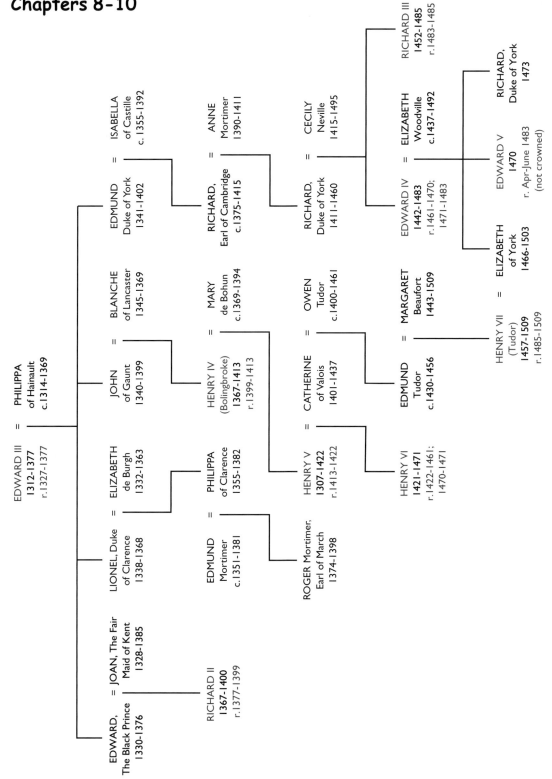

Appendix 3: Willie, Willie, Harry, Ste

And finally…As a way of remembering the kings and queens of England, many of whom you have learnt about in this book, here is an old schoolboy rhyme:

Willie, Willie, Harry, Ste,

Harry, Dick, John, Harry three;

One, two, three Neds, Richard two,

Harrys four, five, six … then who?

Edwards four, five, Dick the bad,

Harrys (twain*), then Ned (the lad);

Mary, Bessie, James the vain,

Charlie, Charlie, James again.

Will and Mary, Anna Gloria,

Georges four, then Will, Victoria;

Edward seven, George and Ted,

George the sixth, now Liz instead.

* Note that twain means two.

Learn this by heart, and you will never forget who ruled when ever again.

Appendix 4: Glossary

Act of Accord – A 1460 agreement between Henry VI and Richard, Duke of York, that the throne would pass to Richard on Henry's death.

alms – Money donated to the poor, usually through begging.

apprentices – Boys who had been bound by their families to learn a trade.

archbishops – Leading **bishops**, of which there were two in England: the Archbishops of Canterbury and York.

assizes – The travelling royal courts encouraged by Henry I.

barbican – A fortified outer gatehouse, set in a **castle** wall.

barons – Important landowners in Normandy.

battering ram – A log with an iron head mounted on wheels, used to pound the castle wall or door.

battle – In battle formation, a block of footsoldiers and **knights**.

battlements – Raised portions at the top of **castle** walls, from which archers could fire down onto attackers.

Bayeux Tapestry – A 70 metre-long embroidered cloth telling the story of the Conquest from the Norman perspective, ordered by William's half-brother Odo of Bayeux.

belfries – Siege towers used by attackers to climb over **castle** walls.

Benedictines – An **order** of **monks** known as 'black monks', with often the wealthiest and most powerful **monasteries** in the country.

besieging – The action of laying **seige** to a **castle** or city.

bishop – A senior churchman in charge of a **diocese**, and based in a **cathedral**.

blood libel – False stories that the Jewish religion allowed murder, usually of Christian children.

breach – A gap caused by a collapse in the **castle** wall through digging by attackers.

bubo – A swelling of the lymph glands in the armpit or groin; an effect of Bubonic Plague.

Carthusians – An **order** of **monks** who were very strict and mostly spent time alone in cells.

castellan – The leading guardian of a **castle**.

castle – A fortified building, used as a base for soldiers to defend land.

cathedral – The leading church of a **diocese**, and the seat of a **bishop**.

Chapter Mass – The 9am service in a **monastery** and **nunnery**.

charter – A legal document giving a town the right to have its own government, laws and taxes.

chastity – The monastic rule of having nothing to do with the opposite sex, including marrying or having children.

chevauchée – A hit-and-run raid practised by English **knights** in France. The intention was to plunder and cause mayhem amongst the enemy.

chivalry – A standard of behaviour that all **lords** and **knights** were expected to reach.

church – A place of Christian worship, and centre of the village community.

Cistercians – An **order** of **monks** known as 'white monks', who tried to abide by rules more strictly than the **Benedictines**.

Cluniacs – An **order** of **monks** who regarded church ceremony as very important.

Compline – The 7pm service in a **monastery** and **nunnery**.

concentric – In **castles**, the pattern of having a circular wall within another circular wall.

coronation – The ceremony where the head of the Church symbolically placed the crown on the head of the new king.

cottars – Peasants with little or no land to farm, holding only a dwelling ('cottage').

croft – A garden at the back of a peasant's dwelling, for growing vegetables and keeping a small number of animals.

crusader states – Areas of the Holy Land that were controlled by Christians, after the successes of previous Crusades.

curfew – A time in the evening when nobody was allowed outside their own houses.

curtain walls – The outer walls of a castle compound, often connected with towers.

cut-purses – Pickpockets. In medieval times people carried their money in a pouch hanging on a piece of string, which could be cut by thieves.

demesne – The land belonging to the **lord** of the **manor**.

diocese – The area of church activity led by a **bishop**.

Domesday Book – A survey of all the land and landholders in England, compiled in 1085-1086.

Dominicans – A monastic order, known as the 'black **friars**'.

drawbar – A bar that could be drawn horizontally across the inside of a **castle** entrance to prevent entry by attackers.

drawbridge – A hinged bridge, connected by chains to a **castle**, that could be raised to prevent entry by attackers.

earls – The holders of most land, after the king, who oversaw the running of the earldoms and were important military leaders.

excommunicate – The action of not allowing someone to take part in church services.

fallow – The action of not sowing crops in a field for the year following harvesting. Animals were often put to graze on the grass and weeds in order to replace the nutrients in the soil.

fealty – The oath of loyalty and promise to defend a lord's (or king's) position in times of war.

Feudal System – A Norman system of military service and tax, based on the amount of land held by each section of society.

flagellants – People who believed that by whipping themselves they would pay penance for mankind's sins, thus stopping the spread of the Plague.

Franciscans – A monastic order, known as the 'grey **friars**'.

freeman – A man at the lowest level of the Feudal System, who had only the minimum of rights.

friars – **Monks** who travelled, preaching and begging, rather than living in a **monastery** of their own.

fyrd – The soldiers of lower rank in the English (Saxon) army, bound to provide two months of military service every year.

guild – An organisation of craftsmen set up to protect them and their work.

guildhalls – The headquarters of a **guild**. Usually these could only be afforded by the largest and richest guilds.

habit – A robe worn by **monks**.

Harrying of the North – The burning of lands in Yorkshire in 1069, in retaliation for a Northern rebellion. Thousands are supposed to have died of hunger due to their crops being destroyed.

heresy – A belief that goes against the authority of the Church.

Hereward the Wake – An English rebel leader, based in East Anglia. After the Conquest he became a heroic, almost mythical figure.

High Mass – The 11am service in a **monastery** and **nunnery**.

hoarding – A wooden construction that projected from a **castle** wall, allowing archers to fire down onto attackers.

homage – The act of swearing fealty to a lord (or king), and becoming their **vassal**.

housecarls – The professional, elite soldiers of the English (Saxon) army.

hue and cry – An alert raised when a crime was committed. Everybody who heard the 'hue and cry' was expected to help to pursue the criminal.

indenture – The agreement under which a boy was contracted to become an **apprentice**.

interdict – The action of not allowing church services to be held at all.

journeyman – A worker who had served an apprenticeship and could thus be paid for his work by the **master craftsman**.

knights – Cavalry soldiers who fought on horseback with lances.

Lollards – A movement founded by John Wycliff. They believed that the Bible should be read in a person's native language, and did not support the authority of the Pope.

longbow – The bow favoured by English archers. It could fire much more rapidly than the crossbow, but with a shorter range.

lord – One who had **vassals** under the Feudal System.

Lords Appellant – A group of nobles who rebelled against Richard II and ran the country for a year after the Merciless Parliament of 1388.

Magna Carta – The 'Great Charter' endorsed by King John at Runnymede in 1215.

mail – Or 'chain mail' or 'ring mail', a protective vest made of metal loops woven together.

mangonel – An ancient device for throwing stones, more compact than a **trebuchet**.

manor – The unit of farming, which consisted of a village, fields, woods, meadows and sometimes a **manor house**.

manor house – A house belonging to the **lord**, though not always inhabited by him.

master craftsman – A worker who took on an **apprentice** to teach, feed and clothe.

Matins – The midnight service in a **monastery** and **nunnery**, lasting about an hour.

mayor – The leading citizen of a town or city.

moat – A deep ditch surrounding a **castle**, filled with water.

monasteries – An establishment of **monks** belonging to a particular **order**.

monks – Men who gave up all their possessions to live in a **monastery** and abide by the rules of their **order**.

motte and bailey – A type of Norman castle, easily and quickly constructed. The **motte** was a mound of earth; the **bailey** was the enclosure surrounding it.

murder holes – Holes in the ceiling of a **castle** entrance. Boiling oil could be poured through them onto the heads of attacking soldiers, as could water to put out fires.

mystery and miracle plays – Religious plays, often paid for by a **guild**.

nobles – The richest and most powerful men in England. These included **earls** and other major landowners.

Nones – The 2pm service in a **monastery** and **nunnery**.

nunnery – An establishment of **nuns** belonging to a particular **order**.

nuns – Women who gave up all their possessions to live in a **nunnery** and abide by the rules of their **order**.

obedience – The monastic rule of following God's will through the Church leaders.

obituary – A written summary of a person's life, made after his death.

ordeal – A manner of trial at which the accused would have to prove his innocence 'in the eyes of God'. This could be done with trial by fire, water or combat.

orders – Groups of **monks** and **nuns** with different interpretations of the Benedictine rules.

pageant – A procession, often paid for by a **guild**.

Parliament – The council of **barons** formed after Henry III swore to uphold the Provisions of Oxford in 1258.

pilgrim – A person who travels to a place of special relevance to his religious belief.

pillory – A punishment where the legs of the offender were locked in place.

plate armour – Armour made with plates of steel; heavier than **mail** but providing better protection.

pogroms – Attacks on Jewish people or businesses.

Poll Tax – A general tax payable by all citizens, first imposed in 1377.

Poor Clares – The most popular **order** of **nuns**, founded in 1215.

Pope – The head of the Christian Church, usually based in Rome. Popes claimed to have inherited their authority directly from St. Peter.

portcullis – A spiked iron gate that could drop down in front of a **castle** entrance to prevent entry by attackers.

pottage – A thick soup of vegetables and sometimes meat.

poverty – The monastic rule of owning no possessions.

Prime – The 6am service in a **monastery** and **nunnery**.

propaganda – Material that encourages people to think a certain way, usually for a political purpose.

relics – Objects that were supposed to hold some religious significance.

sagas – Entertaining stories about kings and gods; a Scandinavian tradition.

schiltrons – In battle formation, a block of footsoldiers.

scutage – A war tax imposed by King John.

serfs – See **villeins**.

shell keep – A keep that was usually round and designed to enclose the buildings that needed to be defended.

shieldwall – A line of soldiers with shields locked closely together.

siege – A blockade of a city or **castle**.

solar – The private room of a **lord** and his family within a **castle**.

Statute of Labourers – A 1351 law that forced peasants to accept the wages and conditions of work that applied before the Plague in 1348.

statutes – Acts of law passed by **Parliament**.

stocks – A punishment where the arms and head of the offender were locked in place.

tenants-in-chief – The most important landowners, who paid **homage** and swore **fealty** directly to the king.

timber-framed – Made from a frame of wooden beams.

tithes – Taxes raised by the Church.

tolls – A payment charged to people wanting to pass a certain point on a road.

tonsure – The partial shaving of a **monk's** head.

tower keep – A keep built as a tower that housed the inhabitants of the **castle**.

trebuchet – A medieval device for throwing large boulders, flaming objects and diseased animals. Larger and more powerful than a **mangonel**.

usury – The action of lending money for profit. The medieval church believed this to be wrong.

vassal – One who swore **fealty** and paid **homage** to a lord (or king), and received land in return.

Vespers – The 4pm service in a **monastery** and **nunnery**.

villeins – Peasants with land to farm. Villeins were unable to leave their **manor**. See also **serfs**.

watchmen – Guardians of the town who patrolled the streets at night and kept watch on the defensive walls.

wattle-and-daub – A system of building where branches and twigs were woven into the gaps of a wooden frame, then covered with plaster.

wimple – A hood worn by **nuns**.

witan – The council of the most important men in England, including **earls** and **bishops**.

yeoman – A farmer who owned his own land.

Index